THE MORAL IMAGINATION

THE MORAL IMAGINATION

Essays on Literature and Ethics

By Christopher Clausen

UNIVERSITY OF IOWA PRESS
Iowa City

University of Iowa Press, Iowa City 52242
Printed in the United States of America
First edition, 1986

Book and jacket design by Sandra Strother Hudson
Typesetting by G & S Typesetters, Inc., Austin, Texas
Printing and binding by Edwards Brothers, Inc., Ann Arbor, Michigan

Library of Congress Cataloging-in-Publication Data

Clausen, Christopher, 1942–
The moral imagination.

Includes index.
1. Literature and morals.   2. Literature, Modern—
19th century—History and criticism.   3. Literature,
Modern—20th century—History and criticism.   I. Title.
PN49.C57   1987   809'.93353   86-11282
ISBN 0-87745-151-6

For

N. P. C.

Then there's the ones what honestly don't know,
they don't grasp as there's rules at all, if you follow
me. That sort never get very far, cause of not
understanding what makes anyone else tick. They
can be quite brainy, but they're thick with it. Morally
thick, if you follow.

PETER DICKINSON,
One Foot in the Grave

The author of a work of imagination is trying to
affect us wholly, as human beings, whether he
knows it or not; and we are affected by it, as human
beings, whether we intend to be or not.

T. S. ELIOT,
"Religion and Literature"

Contents

Preface

THERE IS no such thing as a moral or an immoral book," announced Oscar Wilde, echoing Poe, nearly a century ago. "Books are well written, or badly written. That is all." To put the relation of literature to ethics in these terms is to deny, or more likely overlook, the bearing that the moral shallowness or profundity of a book might have on whether, all things considered, it is well or badly written. Most critics will agree that good writing is more than a question of style and structure. Still, many critics today would agree with Wilde's formulation, which has come to represent one of the more visceral attitudes of twentieth-century literary study. The fact that Wilde made his remarks in the preface to one of the few successful moral allegories of modern times, *The Picture of Dorian Gray,* is an irony that usually goes unnoticed.

The nine essays in this book consider some approaches that writers of poetry and fiction have taken towards representing moral judgments in imaginative literature and some ways in which critics can appropriately respond. My concerns are both rhetorical and thematic. Dividing my attention almost evenly between fiction and poetry, I have chosen to include popular as well as "elite" literature, not only because it exerts a more widespread influence on attitudes but because our moral expectations, like our esthetic ones, vary widely with different genres. We do not expect the characters in a children's story to behave the same way, or be judged by the same standards, as those in a tragedy, a crime novel, a fantasy, or a lyric poem. Exploring these differences is an essential step towards understanding how the moral imagination manifests itself. That it does manifest itself in all of them is hard to deny. As Anthony Boucher, a contemporary critic of detective fiction, points out, "It is all but impossible for any writer above the hack level to write about people and problems without implying some set of values, some ethical standard." That has certainly been true throughout the nineteenth and twentieth centuries, a time of individualism in literature as in much else.

Readers of this book will find some unexpected but deliberate juxtapositions of authors—of Andrew Marvell with Lewis Carroll, Mark Twain with Kenneth Grahame, Arthur Conan Doyle with his heir-of-sorts J. R. R. Tolkien. They will also find, I hope, a conception of the moral imagination that acquires a credible coherence as Padraic Pearse and Czeslaw Milosz illuminate each other across the decades and some retrospective light is shed on Robert Frost by the activities of three successors in the attempt to make poetic sense out of being American. The book proposes no general theory of the relations between literature and ethics. For reasons given in the first chapter, I think such a theory would be unprofitable. A revived criticism that employs ethical criteria is unlikely to be as systematic as the more theoretical kinds of criticism that dominate many graduate schools today. Nor will it be as peremptory in its notions of what constitutes good and bad as the older moral criticism of Dr. Johnson, who declared that "it is always a writer's duty to make the world better," or his less confident successor Matthew Arnold.

The classical and Christian belief in norms (not merely averages) of human conduct that are universally valid, and hence in a literature organized around those norms, has no longer enough cultural authority to support a revival of Johnsonian criticism. History and anthropology have largely discredited such absolute notions of behavior. That fact does not mean ethics is out of date; quite the contrary, it ought to make people more conscious and reflective about moral questions and to make the ethical content of literature (and of criticism) more valued, if less doctrinaire. Whatever kind of ethics and literature we want, only the very thoughtless believe that we can dispense with either one or the other. Literary works usually embody moral problems and reflect moral attitudes, sometimes even moral theories. There is no good reason for criticism to tiptoe around one of the major reasons that some literary works endure.

The effort of bringing an undogmatic moral criticism back to life, or rather of showing that it was only playing dead, is worthwhile for a number of reasons. The most important for literary purposes is that we should be clearer about what we are doing when we judge a book to be well or badly written. What follows is a discussion of that complicated question, together with some examples—varied but far from exhaustive—of how the views put forward in chapter 1 might be applied to the subject matter of all literary theories, the diverse world of actual poems, novels, and plays. My own ethical assumptions should be obvious as we go along.

EARLIER VERSIONS of eight of these essays have appeared, some of them in very different form, in the following magazines: "Morality, Poetry, and Criticism," *Kenyon Review;* "Death and Two Maidens," *Sewanee Review;* "Home and Away," *Children's Literature;* "Sherlock Holmes, Order, and the Late-Victorian Mind," *Georgia Review;* "Robert Frost's Marriage Group," *New England Review;* "Padraic Pearse: The Revolutionary as Artist," *Shaw Review;* "Czeslaw Milosz: The Exile as Californian," *Literary Review;* "Explorations of America," *Verse* (Oxford).

For reading and giving advice on one or more chapters, I should like to thank George Core, Quentin L. Gehle, Stanley W. Lindberg,

Johann A. Norstedt, Samuel F. Pickering, Jr., Wyatt Prunty, John Taggart, James L. W. West, III, and Stanley Weintraub. My greatest debt is to my wife, Nancy Clausen.

I am grateful to Virginia Polytechnic Institute and State University and to The Pennsylvania State University for secretarial and other kinds of help from which I have profited while writing, revising, and preparing this book for publication. Special thanks are due to Betsy Webb and Kim Cooper, who wrestled the manuscript through a recalcitrant computer.

1. Morality, Poetry, and Criticism

DESPITE THE COMMON RECOGNITION in recent years that literary criticism is in some significant ways a philosophical inquiry, discussions of literature and ethics make most contemporary critics squirm in their chairs. The largely dismissive response that greeted John Gardner's *On Moral Fiction* when it came out in 1978 was a notable example of this unease. If fiction can be reputably described as moral or immoral, one fear goes, less reputable forces, from Stalinism to fundamentalism, may use these descriptions for purposes that few literary critics would approve. The logical consequence of moral criticism, whether exerted from the right, the left, or no obvious political standpoint, is widely if unreflectively assumed to be censorship. The group that calls itself the Moral Majority, as one distinguished critic recently reminded us, is not noted for the catholicity of its tastes.[1] Since *moral* can easily mean narrow, bigoted, intolerant, let us see that the word and concept remain banished from the vocabulary of reputable criticism. So runs one train of thought.

There are other reasons for the reluctance of most critics in the last forty years to engage openly in any kind of criticism that uses morality as a criterion for evaluation. (I shall use the word *morality* broadly to include both how we should treat others and what goods an individual or society should pursue.) Since the attitudes that underlie these objections are widespread among adherents of

1

many different schools or none, it would be for the most part su-
pererogatory to attach names or labels to them. One is the superstition that esthetic categories are more intrinsic to the nature of
literature than ethical or cognitive ones. I. A. Richards speaks for
many who are by no definition New Critics in declaring, "It is
never what a poem *says* which matters, but what it *is*."[2] Literature
is an art, the argument goes; a work of art is to be judged by esthetic criteria that inhere in it, not by nonesthetic ones dragged in
from outside. Or, as Cleanth Brooks, again expressing a view that
has been widely shared beyond the bounds of his own critical
school, put it in an influential formulation, "A poem, then . . . is
to be judged, not by the truth or falsity as such, of the idea which
it incorporates, but rather by its character as drama—by its coherence, sensitivity, depth, richness, and tough-mindedness."[3] That
at least four of these five criteria are ethical—"extrinsic" criteria
disguised as "intrinsic" ones—is evident, a fact which suggests
two reasons for describing the "intrinsic" view as a superstition.

One is that a moral interpretation of experience is usually as
demonstrably present in an important literary work as is form.
Where it is, no critic as good as Cleanth Brooks ignores it as part
of his basis for evaluation in practice, whatever his theory may
say. On the whole, we expect great poets' and novelists' interpretations of life to stand up, as interpretations, to the most
searching examination. We may find them in large measure true
and profound, or false but profound, or true but shallow (that is,
platitudes), or both false and shallow. In any of these cases, we
are evaluating thought; in the last two, we are no longer talking
about great writers. (It is, of course, the second case that raises
the greatest problems for moral criticism.) If quality of thought
were not a major element in our evaluation, the formally elegant
works of Landor would rank higher in critical esteem than the
frequently clumsy ones of Wordsworth; Poe, who eschewed ethical and intellectual content, would be a better poet than the awkward Hardy; and Harold Robbins would be a greater novelist than

Theodore Dreiser. Often the morality of a literary work is so com-
monplace that we overlook it in making our evaluation. In other
cases, critics are taken by surprise when the ethical content of an
established work gives rise to extra-academic debate. Recent public controversy over the merits of *Huckleberry Finn* centered entirely on the moral question of whether the book condemned or
condoned slavery and racism. Those who attacked the book were
mistaken in their interpretation of it; they were by no means
wrong in identifying an important basis for evaluating it. As this
episode suggests, it is time that a sophisticated, properly analytical moral criticism become once again a respectable activity.

A related reason for skepticism towards the "intrinsic" view of
literature is that whatever we decide about the nature and meaning of a given work, our standards for evaluating it always come
from outside it. Consciously or unconsciously, we are always
measuring it against other works and/or an abstract set of demands. It is reasonable to require that our standards of evaluation
be appropriate to the nature of the work (we do not judge *Macbeth*
by the standards of scholarly history), but as we have already
seen, the nature of a literary work may be conceived in several
ways, and it is not at all obvious that the esthetic is usually the
most important. Many kinds of works travel under the banner of
"literature" or "poetry," and no single standard is equally useful
for all. "Philosophical" criticism usually seeks to discover and formulate the general laws of a total system called literature, poetry,
narration, and so on. To doubt publicly that there *is* any such system exposes one to the charge of being empirical, amateurish,
gentlemanly, British, unphilosophical, or naive (all of these presumably being synonyms). Still, it seems inescapable that any
theory of literature, or of any branch of literature, has to be em-
pirically based on actual works, not simply on other theories
about language. Our knowledge of poetry comes from reading
poems; our criteria for understanding and judging a poem come
from our systematized observation of other poems and from our

knowledge of life, which comes in turn from an infinity of sources, of which philosophy is one. In any event, the poem itself will not tell us how to evaluate it.[4]

Another basis for the reluctance of many critics to consider (openly at least) the moral aspects of literary works is the desire to stay on the safe side of the fact-value chasm. If criticism is to be as rigorous as possible, this argument runs, it should confine itself to questions that are amenable to logic and evidence and, in principle, consensus. In the twentieth century, at least, neither writers nor critics exhibit any consensus as to what moral values are important or "correct." (That the quotation marks around the last word are not likely to strike most readers as odd is a strong indication of the moral relativism that most educated people take for granted today.) To base any part of the evaluative function of criticism on such subjective criteria, it is alleged, is either to wander in speculation or to enclose oneself in dogma. Where F. R. Leavis and Yvor Winters rushed in, most later critics have feared to tread.

There are at least three answers to this reluctance. The first, and perhaps least interesting, is the possibility that the breakdown of moral consensus in the post-Renaissance world has been much exaggerated. No individual or society, however original, starts from zero on ethical questions. Since such a statement cannot possibly be proved, I merely offer the suggestion that there is far more agreement today on private moral values than it is at all fashionable to believe, and pass on to other matters. The second reason for not evading in theory a moral judgment that often cannot be avoided in practice is that the distinction between a fact and a value is not nearly as clear as it once was; as a universal principle, it begins to look like another superstition. It is odd that literary critics, of all people, should ever have accepted such a bifurcation of discourse. That many have done so is perhaps a symptom of the desire, which I have already mentioned, that criticism should become more conceptual and systematic. The desire is a reasonable one, and I share it. Yet readers of literature, even more than philosophers of science, should have been guarded against such an error by the nature of their subject. When Dickens calls attention to the poverty and misery of the English working class, is he making a factual statement (however complicated) or expressing a value? Dr. Johnson, at the end of "The Vanity of Human Wishes," declares that

> These goods for man the laws of Heaven ordain,
> These goods He grants, who grants the power to gain;
> With these celestial Wisdom calms the mind,
> And makes the happiness she does not find.

Is this an assertion of fact (whether true or not) or a statement of value? The question is worth pursuing only as an inoculation against the belief that such distinctions are always possible or important. As Wayne Booth points out, "In the last decade or so, philosophers in great numbers have rediscovered what almost all philosophers until the nineteenth century believed: that there is no implacable barrier between fact statements and value statements, or between what 'is' and what 'ought to be.'"[5] Assertions of value can be profitably argued with logic and evidence, and often are so argued; the history of any discipline is filled with examples of such arguments.

The third and most important reason for denying that the uncertainty of moral judgments should deter critics from invoking them is that such a proscription would apply equally to moral philosophers, juries, members of legislative bodies, or any other group of people who are concerned with questions of ethics. As an objection, it lacks force, for as long as the universe contains conscious beings whose willed actions cause themselves and each other many kinds and degrees of suffering and joy, moral questions will remain inescapably important. It is precisely those sufferings and joys, together with their causes and consequences, that provide the central subject matter of poetry and fiction. The fact that not all writers come to conclusions that can be reconciled simply means that literature, like life itself, is various—if it were otherwise, one book would suffice—not that its practitioners need not be taken with full seriousness when they treat of ethical matters. The question of distinguishing true values from false, or values that we ought to respect from those we ought not, is in principle no different in poetry than in any other form of discourse.[6] Nor can it be settled by merely historical criteria, however useful history is in helping us get at a work's meaning. (Knowing about Greek heroic and esthetic ideals will not by itself enable us to judge either Achilles or *The Iliad.*) We have to take the work as a whole and decide how well, using the various resources of poetic language, an author makes his or her case. To do so is not to ignore poetry as art. It is rather to recognize that most important poems are at least partly moral in tenor, and that where this is so the assertions of poetry, whether directly or indirectly made, should be taken seriously as assertions, not evaded by references to their function in a dramatic or esthetic structure. The ordering imagination is usually, among other things, a moral imagination.

As is well known, few poets or critics denied the instructive functions of literature before the middle of the nineteeth century. Didacticism was not merely *a* respectable view of poetic purposes; it was (when coupled with delight, in a formulation that went back to Horace) virtually the *only* respectable view. It is important to emphasize here that the two elements are only analytically separate; in a successful literary work, instruction and esthetic delight are one thing—instruction delights, or what is delightful instructs. Sir Philip Sidney restated the position memorably in declaring the poet to be "the right popular philosopher" who through precept and example, showing and telling, teaches "the knowledge of a man's self, in the ethic and politic consideration, with the end of well-doing, and not of well-knowing only."[7] Like Sidney in the sixteenth century, Johnson in the eighteenth ranked poetry as a more important form of knowledge than science because of its ethical content:

> But the truth is, that the knowledge of external nature, and the sciences which that knowledge requires or includes, are not the great or the frequent business of the human mind. . . . Prudence and Justice are virtues and excellences of all times and of all places; we are perpetually moralists, but we are geometricians only by chance. Our intercourse with intellectual nature is necessary; our speculations upon matter are voluntary, and at leisure. . . .
>
> Those authors, therefore, are to be read at schools that supply most axioms of prudence, most principles of moral truth, and most materials for conversation; and these purposes are best served by poets, orators, and historians.[8]

And Wordsworth, at the end of *The Prelude,* avows a similarly didactic purpose for his own and Coleridge's future careers as poets:

> . . . what we have loved,
> Others will love, and we will teach them how;
> Instruct them how the mind of man becomes
> A thousand times more beautiful than the earth
> On which he dwells. . . .

This sense of mission follows naturally from the Preface to *Lyrical Ballads,* where Wordsworth had earlier proclaimed: "Aristotle, I have been told, hath said, that poetry is the most philosophic of all writing: it is so: its object is truth, not individual and local, but general. . . . Poetry is the image of man and nature." Whether or not Wordsworth's understanding of Aristotle is correct, this view of poetry was widely shared by poets, critics, and ordinary readers until the twentieth century.

As René Wellek and Austin Warren, who gave currency to the extrinsic/intrinsic formulation, plausibly point out, "From views that art is discovery or insight into truth, we should distinguish the view that art—specifically literature—is propaganda, the view, that is, that the writer is not the discoverer but the per-

7

suasive purveyor of the truth."[9] This distinction is not always easy to apply in practice (how would one apply it to Dante?), but at least it recognizes that some kinds of truth are intrinsic to literature. Poetic truth is not usually capable of scientific verification. In a less formal sense, however, poets and good readers alike test it constantly against their total knowledge and experience of life. What better principle of verification have we for most of the truths on which we base our most important decisions?

IT WOULD BE easy to quote authorities almost endlessly, from Plato to Matthew Arnold to John Gardner, on the moral responsibilities of poetry—either poetry narrowly defined, or poetry in the pre–nineteenth-century sense of the word as including drama and prose fiction. I doubt, however, that it would be very useful. Much theoretical criticism has always suffered from the suspicion that it has lost touch with actual literary works, that it talks abstractly at length about what poems should do or must do without stopping often enough to examine what poems actually do. The history of criticism is replete with statements that their famous authors would never have made had they stopped to think about the examples and counterexamples that might bear on the question. Before talking further about the theoretical relations of poetry and ethics, therefore, I should like to examine some well-known short poems—the most obviously esthetic kind of literary works—to see how they treat ethical questions. The equivocal meaning of *how* in the previous sentence is well worth noticing, for it is closely related to the questions of ends and means I have been dealing with by way of introduction. *How* in this case means two things. First, by what techniques have the authors of relatively short poems, who unlike the novelists have little in the way of plot and characterization to work with, rendered moral concepts and conflicts? Second, how important, and how persuasive, are moral concepts in some highly regarded poems that (with one exception) most readers today would not regard as objectionably didactic? Having completed this exercise, we may be in a better position to see what further generalizations on morality in poetry and the moral criticism of literature suggest themselves.

Let us begin in the seventeenth century with a poem that has often inspired technical analysis, Donne's "Valediction Forbidding Mourning." This poem has been so highly praised in the twentieth century that we are justified in wondering whether its claims on us are merely those of skillful artistry. A skillful poem it certainly is. In a series of four famous metaphors ranging from the deaths of virtuous men to the coordinated feet of a drawing compass, Donne proposes that the partings of those who genuinely love should be silent, without tears, invisible to the world. The poem ends with the most celebrated simile in English poetry (celebrated in part because it seems so improbable): the woman as the fixed foot of the compass, the man on his voyage as the foot that makes the circle:

> Such wilt thou be to me, who must
> Like the other foot, obliquely run;
> Thy firmness makes my circle just,
> And makes me end where I begun.

The seemingly far-fetched figure works splendidly. Donne has plotted the progress of his poetic thought so well that the transition from one metaphor to another creates little difficulty for the reader who has become at all familiar with this kind of poetry. The "Valediction" amply deserves the technical praise it has received.

And yet to elucidate the manner of this poem's success is only to begin to criticize it. The famous metaphors, the twists and turns of technique, are after all used in the service of expressing a moral ideal. "As virtuous men pass mildly away . . . So let us melt, and make no noise. . . ." *Why?* What is the importance of this calm parting that the poet so skillfully and insistently recommends? How seriously can and do we as readers take the idea that is at the heart of all this virtuosity? It is by no means obvious that lovers ought to suppress their emotions on parting. To do so violates the popular Freudianism of the twentieth century and the emotional style of love in our time, as a glance at the sidewalks in front of any college dormitory on the last day of school will plainly attest. Why does Donne advocate something so apparently unnatural as a public show of indifference between lovers, and in reading the poem are we likely to be persuaded that he is right?

The explanation comes in the fourth and fifth stanzas of the poem, where Donne makes it explicit:

> Dull sublunary lovers' love
> (Whose soul is sense) cannot admit
> Absence, because it doth remove
> Those things which elemented it.

> But we by a love so much refined
> That our selves know not what it is,
> Inter-assurèd of the mind,
> Care less, eyes, lips, and hands to miss.

Lust that masquerades as love requires the constant presence of physical stimulation; in the body's absence, there is nothing to keep it going. True love is higher than this, and the physical separation of the lovers does not change or diminish it. Thus, spiritual lovers need not be together, and to protest overmuch at parting would suggest to the world that their love is of the merely physical variety. In the kinds of love there is a hierarchy. Donne not merely recommends the highest but (in what may be an imaginary dramatic situation) seeks to assure the object of his love that theirs is of that kind.

I suspect few people in the twentieth century believe that kinds of attraction between men and women can be distinguished as

10

Donne distinguishes them here, and probably fewer still of the admirers of the poem would be happy to think of themselves in such a situation as "gold to airy thinness beat." There is little reason to think that seventeenth-century readers were appreciably different in this respect. Yet poems of merely technical facility do not usually receive the acclaim of "A Valediction Forbidding Mourning." What is it that really attracts us so much in this poem?

I suggest that it is an ideal of dignity which, no matter how little intention we have of practicing it personally, we nonetheless feel to be an important and permanent virtue that receives one of its most memorable expressions here. For the lovers to part as Donne recommends, which is a corollary of loving as he recommends, dignifies them. They come to exemplify one of the better choices that human beings can make. Such behavior is more than simply a question of good form; it becomes the outward and visible sign of an inward and spiritual grace. Thus the technique of a great artist makes possible a moral statement that readers in a later century, however they wish to formulate the matter, find moving and penetrating. The advantage of poetry as a medium for moral thought is that it can express ideas more subtly and precisely than prose. The poet may start with an old idea, like dignity or spiritual love, but when he has finished with it, usually it is something more than it was when he began. This transformation is due partly to the resources of poetic language; it is also what writers who are vigorous thinkers commonly do with ideas. And as Coleridge pointed out, great poets are usually vigorous thinkers.

Probably this kind of poem is more to the taste of modern readers than poetry that exhorts its readers more directly. The latter kind, however, has been important in English literature until recently, and the current unpopularity of works such as Johnson's "Vanity of Human Wishes," from which I have already quoted, may be a temporary phase in the history of taste. Didacticism comes in more shapes than many twentieth-century critics have cared to recognize, and as a basis for negative evaluation it is as extrinsic as any other criterion; what grounds are there for saying that poets should not do what good poets have done so often? Still, Johnson's neoclassical poem, with its abstractness, its personifications, and its moral exhortation, is an excellent example of a kind of work that most twentieth-century readers have not cared for, and a brief examination of the way in which these technical features serve a moral purpose may be instructive.

Johnson's habit of moral generalization is evident in the first lines of the poem:

> Let Observation, with extensive view,
> Survey mankind, from China to Peru . . .

—survey mankind, that is, with the purpose of demonstrating the folly and irrationality of its members.

> How rarely Reason guides the stubborn choice,
> Rules the bold hand, or prompts the suppliant voice;
> How nations sink, by darling schemes oppressed,
> When Vengeance listens to the fool's request.

These lines are the thesis that Johnson sets out to prove by examples from history. Cardinal Wolsey falls from power to disgrace and death; Buckingham is assassinated at the height of his glory; in some of the most often quoted lines of the poem, Charles XII, the conqueror-king of Sweden, loses his life in a trivial skirmish:

> His fall was destined to a barren strand,
> A petty fortress, and a dubious hand;
> He left the name at which the world grew pale,
> To point a moral or adorn a tale.

Further examples and reflections on the capriciousness of fortune ensue, until finally Johnson asks:

> Where then shall Hope and Fear their objects find?
> Must dull Suspense corrupt the stagnant mind?

Must helpless man, in ignorance sedate,
Roll darkling down the torrent of his fate?

No, concludes Johnson, not quite. A theistic stoicism is our best refuge, indeed our only refuge in a world where things usually go wrong. With "Obedient passions, and a will resigned," we can pray, and then accept what happens as the will of God; faith, hope, and love remain to us, although our hope needs to be of a very patient sort. It is through these virtues that "celestial Wisdom calms the mind, / And makes the happiness she does not find."

This conclusion represents one of the major ways in which human beings from ancient times to the present have tried to make sense of life. It is morally impressive. And yet there is something about the poem as a whole that prevents one reader, at least, from assenting to it as warmly as he would like. It is not, somehow, a *friendly* poem, and some formal problems seem to follow from the particular moral ideas that it embodies. What is the trouble?

Much of Johnson's procedure can be defended. The use of abstractions and personified virtues is not in itself a fault. Ethical values are always abstract, impersonal, transcending individuals; presenting them in all their abstractness is one of the major ways in which poets have written moral poems. Milton, Dryden, and Gray are three of the many poets who have done so successfully and who were available to Johnson as models. The merely personal quickly degenerates into the private and the trivial, a fact that is responsible for the banality of much twentieth-century verse. (It is only fair to add that much of the banality to be found in eighteenth- and nineteenth-century verse is due to the opposite flaw, a desire to be edifying to the neglect of anything else.) Literary art typically measures the real against the ideal, the actual against the moral, demonstrating and testing their infinite possible relationships. "A fictitious episode is a compromise be-

13

tween a particular fact and a general assertion," as Laurence Lerner puts it.[10] According to one definition, bad art is art that gives inadequate weight to either the fact or the assertion. This formulation does not require either that the poem be "realistic" in the conventional sense of that term or (the other end of the spectrum) that the poet begin with an abstract idea—although if the poem is "true," the idea will nonetheless be seen to have been there from the start. Take out the ideal element (which is often implied rather than stated), and the main significance of the work as an interpretation of experience has been lost; take out (or inadequately represent) the real world and real people, and the abstract idea remains an inert proposition. The abstract virtue must, as Sidney said, be seen operating in a real context for the literary work to be effective. The old word for plot is *argument,* and it is through plot that the author of a narrative work argues for the correctness of his moral vision. (That plot also serves important purposes unrelated to moral significance, I have no wish to deny.)

The trouble with "The Vanity of Human Wishes" is that it has neither the developed plot and characters of a narrative work nor the unified impact of a lyric. It contains too many discrete examples of human failure, and we feel that Johnson's interest in his characters is minimal; they are illustrations that never attain the status of being fully human. Plenty of famous characters in literature, from Achilles to Sherlock Holmes, are undeveloped and few readers complain. Here, however, Johnson disposes of each character and hustles us on to the next so rapidly that we never care much about the fates of any of them. The fundamental problem is not the abstractness of the virtues and the defects they represent, nor is it the exhortatory tone of the poem. It is that we never become sufficiently intimate with the real context in which those abstractions are supposed to operate. The poem falls short of complete success because it does not persuade us that the world it describes is our own.

We live in a society today that has become so enamored of the

14

personal and concrete, so suspicious of the ideal, that we can no longer read a poem like "The Vanity of Human Wishes" in the way that its author intended. The fault is partly ours; it is also partly inherent in Johnson's method of writing a moral poem. The danger to which he succumbs is, furthermore, inherent in his view of life. The partial failure, which was not inevitable, derives from the form's too faithfully embodying the conclusion that human beings are largely powerless, unimportant victims of fate.

If we turn to a brief, simple lyric by Emily Dickinson (J.401), we find much greater success in conveying a moral assertion, even though the virtue at issue (egalitarianism) is just as abstract as Johnson's virtues and the characters still more undeveloped. Here the moral point—the hypocrisy and pretentiousness of churchgoing New England ladies—is developed through invective and allusion:

> What Soft—Cherubic Creatures—
> These Gentlewomen are—
> One would as soon assault a Plush—
> Or violate a Star—

The poet here has no more human sympathy for her characters than Johnson had (probably less), but because the point of her scorn is a simple one and the reader is never tempted to sympathize with the "gentlewomen," no difficulty arises. Indeed, we are eager for more abuse.

> Such Dimity Convictions—
> A Horror so refined
> Of freckled Human Nature—
> Of Deity—ashamed—
>
> It's such a common—Glory—
> A Fisherman's—Degree—
> Redemption—Brittle Lady—
> Be so—ashamed of Thee—

15

So much for the New England lady! (Somehow she has gone from plural to singular.) We are so accustomed, as nineteenth- and twentieth-century readers, to identify ourselves with "freckled Human Nature" in contrast to an ideal that we fail to notice when we are tricked into doing just the opposite. For precisely as the lady's moral failure lies in judging others against an (unspecified) ideal, we are judging *her* for her failure to recognize their equality, and we never stop to think that she too partakes of human nature. The poet does to her character exactly what she accuses the character of doing.

And yet somehow the poet gets away with it. The technique of the poem—berating "gentlewomen" from the start for a violation of tolerance, one of the most popular of virtues; describing human nature as merely "freckled" where a more traditional Christian would have written "fallen"; then implying that the lady would have looked down on the apostles, and therefore Christ will be justified in looking down on her at the day of judgment— the technique involves the reader's sympathies so skillfully that in all likelihood he or she will never think to ask what Christ will say to the poet about her own failure of tolerance. (We are clearly not dealing with a dramatized "persona" here whose ironic self-contradiction might be intended.) The reader is, in other words, unlikely to notice the moral contradiction at the center of the poem, particularly if his chief concern is with its rhetorical and esthetic features. The critic who thinks such a contradiction does not matter in poetry may justly be accused of overlooking a central issue in *this* poem.

Moral styles, like literary styles, change from century to century, and a poem need not come to an explicit conclusion in order to have moral significance. In the second half of the twentieth century, the dominant moral style is much more tentative and questioning than in any of the poems I have been talking about so far. Similarly, while some values and virtues have permanent validity, each period has its own favorite moral dilemmas that distinguish it from the period before. An example of a contemporary poem that embodies a contemporary moral dilemma without coming to any overt resolution of it is "Noah's Raven," by W. S. Merwin. Like so many poems in its time, it is fully dramatized, in the sense that the raven (who did not return to the Ark) speaks the whole poem in defense of his actions. In so doing, he becomes a spokesman for a certain state of mind, one in which people refuse to accept responsibilities which, they feel, are alien to their nature. "Why," asks the raven, "should I have returned? / My knowledge would not fit into theirs." The raven senses himself different in essence from those whom he is asked to serve. He feels that, in contrast to Noah and the other passengers on the Ark, the unknown "is my home. / It is always beyond them." In a sense that became familiar in the late 1960s, he has dropped out; he feels no obligation. He is a bird whose superior understanding of the world unfits him to serve his fellow voyagers. This point of view he defends by asserting, "Hoarse with fulfillment, I never made promises." Only the responsibilities we have chosen are real. Obligation is personal and voluntary, not something inherent in social life.

Since the poem presents us with no comment on the bird's attitude, we are free to accept or reject it. If my paraphrase indicates a negative response, I should emphasize that the tone of the poem does not force any such response on the reader. Merwin's poem is entirely objective in that no particular evaluation is implied. (The word *hoarse* in the lines quoted above is perhaps an exception, with its echo of Lady Macbeth.) In that sense, it is a poem that could not easily have been written in any century but the twentieth, when moral questions, like esthetic ones, have come to seem matters of individual taste. That does not make the poem any less moral in its theme, however. Nor does it absolve the reader of the necessity to make up his mind. In our time, such objectivity is one of the chief ways in which the literature of moral problems operates, and sometimes operates as effectively

17

through insight as a more explicit moral literature operated in the past. Showing is after all a form of telling, sometimes (not always) the best form.

My final example, in a very different twentieth-century moral style, is an imaginary one, not because no such poem could exist, but because of a language barrier. Its title is "Inferno: Auschwitz," and it was written (let us suppose) in Berlin in 1944. It is narrated by a young SS officer who, having been wounded in a tank battle on the eastern front, is recuperating at the home of his maternal uncle, Rudolf Höss, the commandant of Auschwitz. With enormous skill and detail, this dramatized narrator describes a vast concentration camp in the spare, suggestive style of Dante. As if aware that four decades later he might be read by deconstructionists, he expresses throughout his consciousness of being a figure in a text that is imitative of an earlier tradition. Through his imagination, the various sectors of the camp become the nine circles of Hell. The chief character in each circle explains to the officer what he has done to merit his punishment. In the first circle, nearest to the crematoria, are the surviving Jews of the Warsaw ghetto. Our narrator, at the end of this complex, tough-minded, tightly unified work, walks out of the camp. It is a clear night in winter. He gazes up into the cold sky, looks on the stars again, and thanks God for having restored a true sense of values to European civilization. Despite the comparative paucity of rhyme-words in German, the terza rima is beautifully handled.

Does anyone doubt that such a poem is possible? Does anyone know how to understand or evaluate it adequately without drawing on the resources of a moral universe that exists outside the poem?

"ART REDISCOVERS, generation by generation, what is necessary to humanness," declares John Gardner. "Criticism restates and clarifies, reenforces the wall."[11] In a tentative way, my examination of five poems (real and imaginary) has illustrated this view of literature, criticism, and ethics. Anyone who is skeptical about my position can of course argue, with some justice, that my selection of poems, diverse as it is, is not sufficiently representative to prove much. In the nature of the case, there can never be a convincing refutation of such an objection. "What would you do," the objector might ask, "with the kind of poem (Poe could provide a good sample) that proclaims its own divorce from moral and intellectual concerns, that is in effect a highly sophisticated game of sounds and emotional connotations?" Since I expressed early in this essay the view that literature is diverse and that no one critical approach is equally appropriate to all works, I am not obliged to show that all poems have moral significance. I am inclined, however, to ask the objector for a list of genuinely major poems that have no significant relation to moral questions. Intellectual or moral profundity alone does not make a poem great or even good, as nearly everyone recognizes; in its absence, however, the most technically brilliant work is apt to be at best minor. "The 'greatness' of literature cannot be determined solely by literary standards," as T. S. Eliot put it, "though we must remember that whether it is literature or not can be determined only by literary standards."[12] Every reader, pencil in hand, can test these generalizations for himself.

Having shown what some poets have done, what do I think critics should do? I have already suggested a good deal of my answer, but some concluding remarks may be useful. For critics to talk endlessly about the necessity to read or criticize poetry "as poetry" simply begs the question of how (and how much) poetry differs from other modes of discourse, and of what features most repay our attention in a given poem. It is by form that poetry is defined and distinguished from what is not poetry, but if we confine our attention to form we relegate poetry to a world of its own. To devote more of our attention to content, in which poetry overlaps with other kinds of discourse, returns it to a larger world. Form is often most profitably viewed as an aspect of content, as

19

the medium through which meaning is shaped and made manifest, rather than content as mere raw material for form. A poem is always an imaginative creation, in one sense a microcosm. Yet insofar as what the poet writes has important relations to the experienced world however conceived—the inescapable context of all texts—those relations become an appropriate subject for criticism. In almost all important poetry, those relations are partly moral, and a judgment on the moral significance of the work is necessary to any thorough consideration of it. The distinction between didactic and nondidactic literary works is more a distinction between two ways of reading than a fact about the works themselves. I have tried to show that there is no good theoretical reason to avoid criticism of the moral content of a literary work, and that to do so often distorts our notion of what the work really is.

Such criticism may take two forms. It may, like other interpretive criticism, elucidate the moral implications of a work, make explicit whatever attitudes and assumptions are implicit, and leave the reader to judge their importance. Or it may evaluate those implications, attitudes, or assumptions within and beyond their immediate literary context, with full attention to the ways in which that context determines and qualifies them, as part of a total evaluation of the work. Both forms of moral criticism have their uses; both raise issues that are not exclusively literary. When carried out responsibly, both dignify literature by taking account of more of its facets than a purely esthetic criticism. Diamonds, after all, are not merely beautiful; they are hard enough to cut glass.

If the demand that we take the moral assertions and implications of poems with full seriousness seems to reduce the differences between poetry and other forms of writing, that may well be a healthy effect. Among other advantages, it is much easier to argue for the importance of poetry and fiction in education if great poems and novels are thought of as embodying permanently important kinds of knowledge than if their production is conceived of as merely a game with words, however complicated and demanding. Much of the value of poems in education, as well as for readers who are not professional critics, derives from the fact that poets are centrally involved in moral exploration, choice, and judgment. For critics to go on maintaining the indeterminacy and nonreferentiality of the esthetic object impoverishes not only criticism but the significance of literature to anyone but a specialist. As George Watson has well said, "It is only because great art is more than a structure and a form that its form and structure are worthy of comment at all."[13]

In a succession of books and articles, E. D. Hirsch has argued for a distinction between "meaning" and "significance" that is useful in both interpretation and evaluation of the kind I am suggesting. As he stated it in 1976,

> "meaning" refers to the whole verbal meaning of a text, and "significance" to textual meaning in relation to a larger context, i.e., another mind, another era, a wider subject matter, an alien system of values, and so on. In other words, "significance" is textual meaning as related to some context, indeed any context, beyond itself.[14]

That the critic's understanding and experience of moral values is a legitimate and important context for defining the significance of a literary work is the substance of my argument. Critics, like poets, may be original moral thinkers or thoroughly derivative in their moral views. Neither the poet nor the critic is an infallible prophet, and it goes without saying that critics can be as morally blind or intolerant as anyone else. Plato and Tolstoy are often cited as exemplifying the dangers of moral criticism, but the risk of error or partiality is unavoidable in any kind of criticism. There is no more need that the critic who dissents from the moral conclusions of a poem should deny it all merit than that the philosopher who (like nearly all modern philosophers) rejects most of Plato's conclusions should think Plato a worthless philosopher, or that the historian who finds Gibbon's assertions about Christianity and the fall of Rome misguided should therefore discard the *Decline and Fall* as a great work of history. The breadth and depth of moral analysis, as of any other kind of thought, are not to be measured only by our acceptance or rejection of its conclusions.

There are many kinds of intolerance, and those critics who insist on irony, myth, or the play of signification have not always avoided them. Estheticism, after all, is itself a moral position. Any critical act is an expression of values, an offering of a context of significance whose application another reader may dispute. Much conservative criticism is overtly or covertly moral. So is most radical and feminist criticism, even if often disguised as ideological critique. The moral attitudes of critics, like those of poets, may have extensive public and political implications, or they may have none at all. The place of moral ideas in literary works is varied, complicated, and worthy of far closer attention than it has recently received. To include in our inevitably mixed set of criteria for evaluating poems a judgment on what their authors assert or imply about how human life should be lived does no violence to poetry. On the contrary, by recognizing in poems a variety of cognitive and philosophical significance that has properly been theirs all along, it reaffirms the status of poetry as an art that illuminates our other acts of living.

2. Death and Two Maidens

MAN," Friedrich Schiller announced to the industrializing world of the late eighteenth century, "only plays when, in the full meaning of the word, he is a man; and he is only completely a man when he plays."[1] Such a norm of human activity may have seemed peculiarly worth defining at a time when the nature of work was undergoing its most drastic revision in history, when the settled farm laborers of yesterday were fast being transformed into the proletariat. Not only work but play was changed almost out of recognition by this mass uprooting. Indeed, play for many almost disappeared for a time as children and adults of both sexes vanished into the mills and mines. Suddenly it was a more obviously grim world in which play came to seem a precious refuge from the public realm, at least to those (like the author of *Hard Times*) whose income was not directly dependent on holding other people's leisure to a minimum. Like everything else, play in its old forms could no longer be taken for granted, in life or literature. The forms in which it could be indulged, the persons who might indulge in it, its moral functions, and its relations to work had all to be redefined.

This was so even in the case of people who might be thought relatively immune to economic change, such as ladies of the comfortable classes. The play of Marvell's preindustrial "Coy Mistress" and her putative lover is revealingly different in conception from that of Lewis Carroll's Alice, a subsequent lady of leisure—different not only in such obvious ways as the ages of the characters and the sexual attitudes of their centuries would suggest, but in the whole orientation towards life that their play, or lack of it, embodies. Both characters are concerned with time, both suspicious about their relation to a world beyond play. One, an adult, seems to have considerable control over the circumstances of her life; the other, a child, is shown as having hardly any. Both are beautiful, or at least attractive; both in some undefined sense doomed. Surprisingly, given the neuroses of her creator and her time, it is Alice who is more genuinely, in Schiller's terms, a man. Explaining why will first require an account of the subtle and complicated relations between play and death.

A. E. Housman, a hundred years after Schiller, tells us late in Alice's century that the only way beauty can be proof against time is by dying young. Further, it must be beauty in the act of play. Throughout the millennia of civilization there have been countless thousands of statues, pictures, mosaics of people taking part in games; only in Housman's century, that age when men worked hardest to forge an identity that could stave off the consciousness of death, did any appreciable vogue arise for celebrating work in art. It was the nineteenth century, beset by the fear of losing control, that began the transformation of play into work by professionalizing sport and turning games into preparation for life. (We may remember that the battle of Waterloo was won—although happily not fought—on the playing fields of Eton; and conversely that Kipling called espionage the Great Game.) In *Homo Ludens,* Johan Huizinga uses the supremely Victorian word *earnest* as the antonym of *play* and declares that its significance

> is defined by and exhausted in the negation of "play"—earnest is simply "not playing" and nothing more. The significance of "play," on the other hand, is by no means defined or exhausted by calling it "not-earnest," or "not-serious." Play is a thing by itself. The play-

24

concept as such is of a higher order than is seriousness. For seriousness seeks to exclude play, whereas play can very well include seriousness.[2]

When work for its own sake is overvalued, art becomes mere decoration, just as leisure becomes no more than a concession to human weakness, an opportunity to reenergize oneself for more work. Of course, the "work ethic" makes the need for art and leisure all the greater, but the understanding of that need declines, so that the result for most people is inferior, mass-produced counterfeits of art and play.

Still, near the end of that work-and-death-haunted century, Housman the classical scholar could congratulate a village athlete ("To an Athlete Dying Young") whose occupation has not come down to us:

> Now you will not swell the rout
> Of lads that wore their honors out,
> Runners whom renown outran,
> And the name died before the man.

To live long is to be surpassed, superseded; and nothing life holds can equal the glory of athletic victory—not at any rate for those whose talents are unsuited to more abstract forms of play. This particular athlete, we may assume, is too young to have become deeply mired in the world of work. He remains, in Housman's terms, innocent and pure. The First World War and its cultural aftermath have made us suspicious of public-school rhetoric, but the association of play, death, and glory in the last lines of the poem conveys the hostility to work, adult life, and material rewards that runs like a counterthread through the Victorian mind:

> So set, before its echoes fade,
> The fleet foot on the sill of shade,
> And hold to the low lintel up
> The still-defended challenge-cup.

25

And round that early-laureled head
Will flock to gaze the strengthless dead,
And find unwithered on its curls
The garland briefer than a girl's.

The association of play with death is one of the oldest themes in literature. The first major Western poem recounts in detail the elaborate games that mourn the death of Patroclus; the first English masterpiece ends with the funeral games of that pre-English king who was, rather unexpectedly, *leodum liðost ond lofgeornost*— kindest to his people and most eager for glory. In the *Mahabharata*, Krishna teaches Arjuna how to overcome his pacific scruples by playing at battle. Play, useless activity engaged in for its own sake and for the sake of enduring praise, is the *only* activity other than religious ritual (which has much in common with play) that has traditionally seemed an appropriate response to the fact of death. Through the play of children, as in Wordsworth's "Immortality Ode" and Yeats's "Among School Children," or the play of adults as in Rilke's Ninth Duino Elegy, modern poets likewise have often celebrated this response. Whether we call it defiance or acceptance, the playful state of mind seems to accomplish something that work—activity carried on for useful reward—can never approach. Useful rewards lose their potency at the brink of the grave; the time spent in pursuing them, in denying or evading the inevitable end, merely brings it closer. (The *Bhagavad-Gita,* more perceptive than some Christian works, maintains that only work pursued as play—without thought or hope of even spiritual reward—has spiritual value.) Play at its most conscious is a recognition of the ultimate futility of work, an acknowledgment of the fact that our only freedom consists in doing things for their own sake, since none of the rewards of labor has any permanent efficacy. Play in this ideal sense is an activity of the enlightened, a realization in action of the abiding truth that because we cannot make our sun stand still, we are free—and only free—to make him run.

The eighteenth and nineteenth centuries valued work, respectability, and sexual abstinence; it can hardly surprise us that the speaker in Marvell's poem has long had a bad press. But he is a wiser and more humane man than he is usually given credit for even today, when sex has come to be recognized as the wellspring of adult play. If we were going to live forever, he tells his somewhat narcissistic lady, we could afford to indulge in all the more or less ridiculous conventions of respectability and courtly love alike. But gallant lover and coy mistress will soon go the way of Paris and Helen; it is idle to pretend that either beauty or virtue can postpone the loss of youth and life itself. (In making this assertion, he is of course availing himself of another convention.) To recognize the most central facts of human existence is neither brutal nor cynical, for on what other basis is freedom possible? Without ever ceasing to play, the speaker is fully in earnest:

> But at my back I always hear
> Time's wingèd chariot hurrying near;
> And yonder all before us lie
> Deserts of vast eternity.
> Thy beauty shall no more be found. . . .

The logical consequence of this realization is—play, for the night is coming. Both parties are interested, and there seem to be no practical barriers.

> Now therefore, while the youthful hue
> Sits on thy skin like morning glow,
> And while thy willing soul transpires
> At every pore with instant fires,
> Now let us sport us while we may. . . .

Apart from fear of pregnancy, the only argument that could render this logic suspect is one based on traditional Christian attitudes towards sexual morality. If there is an afterlife in which God will reward virginity and punish unchastity, then a playful attitude in the face of death is imprudent. Since neither the speaker, the lady (we can judge from the fact that the speaker makes no effort to meet such an argument), nor you, dear reader, entertain such a belief, we may discard it as a scruple. The lover's conclusion is, given the circumstances as the poem conveys them, morally impeccable, intellectually enlightened, and fully consistent with the long tradition (older than *carpe diem*) in which play is seen as the appropriate response to mortality:

> Let us roll all our strength and all
> Our sweetness up into one ball,
> And tear our pleasures with rough strife
> Thorough the iron gates of life:
> Thus, though we cannot make our sun
> Stand still, yet we will make him run.

"The classical tradition of *theatrum mundi*," Richard Sennett maintains in *The Fall of Public Man*, "equated society with theater, everyday action with acting. This tradition thus couched social life in aesthetic terms, and treated all men as artists because all men can act."[3] Whatever the historical complexities of such a theory, it is within this tradition that Marvell's lover conducts himself. Play requires civility, an acceptance of convention, and (if it involves more than one person) an impersonal rhetoric supported by the culture itself. Hence the lover's urbanity, the apparent coolness and lack of involvement that make him seem an unattractive manipulator to readers in a more romantic age. When play becomes a means of proving one's worth or validating one's personality, it ceases to be play. Whether the lady's resistance is itself a form of theatrical convention the poem does not make clear. "Play," says Huizinga, "only becomes possible, thinkable, and understandable when an influx of *mind* breaks down the absolute determinism of the cosmos," a passage which describes the man's situation rather than hers.[4] Like Homer's athletes, however, she achieves a glory that lives after her by participating (even if passively) in a game that makes everything else she might have done (even though fictional) insignificant.

THERE IS no use imagining an adult future for Alice Liddell; her whole point as a literary character is that such a future is unprofitable. By Alice's time the self, like the family, can preserve its integrity only by rebellion or retreat from the public world. "Seven years and six months!" Humpty Dumpty exclaims halfway into *Through the Looking-Glass*. "An uncomfortable sort of age. Now if you'd asked *my* advice, I'd have said 'Leave off at seven'—but it's too late now." To which Alice's response is, "I never ask advice about growing."

> "Too proud?" the other enquired.
> Alice felt even more indignant at this suggestion. "I mean," she said, "that one can't help growing older."
> "*One* can't, perhaps," said Humpty Dumpty; "but *two* can. With proper assistance, you might have left off at seven."[5]

Both the opinion and the proper assistance, one is tempted to retort, were provided by Lewis Carroll, whose real-life interest in Alice waned as she approached adolescence but who playfully immortalized her at the ages of seven (*Alice's Adventures in Wonderland* takes place on her seventh birthday) and seven and a half (*Through the Looking-Glass*). Together, these two books constitute the most telling Victorian attack on earnestness, the world of work, and adult life. What they offer as a countervalue is play in the only form that was readily acceptable to nineteenth-century writers and readers, the play of children.

It is a symptom of the massive cultural changes that had taken place since the seventeenth century that childhood had come to be widely idealized in this fashion. The industrializing adult world, as Wordsworth and Dickens noticed, had become serious beyond all precedent. The languid aristocratic tone of Marvell's milieu had given way to the bourgeois ideals of work, duty, self-sacrifice, the virtuous family. As Sennett puts it:

> The 19th Century bourgeois family attempted to preserve some distinction between the sense of private reality and the very different terms of the public world outside the home. The line between the two was confused, often violated, it was drawn in the erotic sphere by a hand impelled by fear, but at least an attempt was made to maintain the separateness and complexity of different domains of social reality. . . . There was an effort—diseased and destined to collapse, to be sure—to make distinctions between realms of experience, and thus to wrest some form out of a society of enormous disorder and harshness.[6]

We should not be surprised that, from Wordsworth's time onward, a whole literature of nostalgia grew up around children, the one large element in the population whose freedom and frivolity (as interpreted, of course, through adult eyes) remained licensed. Why bother to grow up, the Victorian unconscious seems to say, if the rewards are a lifetime of black suits and dresses, twelve-hour days at factory or office, and sermons twice on Sunday? And large numbers of Victorian children visibly did *not* grow up, which made the image of childhood more poignant still.

The most important form in which Alice encounters this dreary world of work is, naturally enough, education. Her most often repeated dread is of being summoned by adults to lessons. Lessons as Alice experiences them are not merely tedious but utterly senseless.

> "When we were still little," the Mock Turtle went on at last, more calmly, though still sobbing a little now and then, "we went to school in the sea. The master was an old Turtle—we used to call him Tortoise—"
> "Why did you call him Tortoise, if he wasn't one?" Alice asked.
> "We called him Tortoise because he taught us," said the Mock Turtle angrily. "Really you are very dull!"

30

"You ought to be ashamed of yourself for asking such a simple question," added the Gryphon; and then they both sat silent and looked at poor Alice, who felt ready to sink into the earth. (74–75)

That particular paradigm of the discipline by which one becomes an adult is from *Alice's Adventures in Wonderland;* there is worse to come in *Through the Looking-Glass.* The creatures Alice encounters are forever hectoring her like schoolmasters gone mad (or, perhaps, like children who have been foolish enough to emulate schoolmasters).

> "You don't know what you're talking about!" cried Humpty Dumpty. "How many days are there in a year?"
> "Three hundred and sixty-five," said Alice.
> "And how many birthdays have you?"
> "One."
> "And if you take one from three hundred and sixty-five what remains?"
> "Three hundred and sixty-four, of course."
> Humpty Dumpty looked doubtful. "I'd rather see that done on paper," he said. (162–63)

Alice's semiconscious desire in both books is to grow up, perhaps because she fondly supposes that she will then understand the baffling behavior of adults. In both books, the process of attaining this goal is presented as a game—cards in *Alice's Adventures,* chess in *Through the Looking-Glass.* Education is the chief rite of passage; but Alice is no sooner down the rabbit-hole than she begins to question, sensibly enough, how power and wisdom can be reached through such a crazy process. Indeed, thinking about lessons makes her question the goal itself.

> "But then," thought Alice, "shall I *never* get any older than I am now? That'll be a comfort, one way—never to be an old woman—but then—always to have lessons to learn! Oh, I shouldn't like *that!*"
> "Oh, you foolish Alice!" she answered herself. "How can you learn lessons in here? Why, there's hardly room for *you,* and no room at all for any lesson-books!"

31

And so she went on, taking first one side and then the other, and
making quite a conversation of it altogether. . . . (29)

What Matthew Arnold described as the mind's dialogue with itself was not, evidently, reserved for Victorian adults.

The games proceed as Alice carries on through a series of
encounters with quasi-adult creatures, few of whom make any
sense at all. Alice herself remains polite, deferential, but curiously
tough-minded; her unsentimental references to death shock
more than one inhabitant of her dreamworld. Along the way she
witnesses the absurdities of the legal system, monarchy, conventional child-rearing, commerce, and—in fine—the earnest mind
in pursuit of more or less mad goals. Were she not seriously in
pursuit of a goal herself, she would be less vulnerable to the advice and abuse of the creatures she encounters; but as she seeks
to become an adult, she finds herself in a double bind, required to
respond as both child and grownup. To enter the garden in *Alice's
Adventures*, for example, she must in rapid succession be large
enough to remove the key from a high table and small enough to
fit through a tiny door. It is hardly surprising that in the early
chapters she repeatedly wonders who she is. Not until she has
reached her goals—in dream, remember—and awakened from
their hollowness can she fully become the playful, liberated child
her creator intended her to be.

As it happens, both books end in precisely this fashion, with
Alice reaching her goal. In each case the dream turns to nightmare, she rebels against the creatures that surround her, and she
awakes—to find herself still safe on her side of the line that di-
vides the humble childish world of play from the pompous adult
world of work. Both times, Alice's rebellion results from her seeing
through the pretensions of the adult world, renouncing for the
moment her childish deference, and freely asserting herself. The
childlike imagination, in short, rises against the conventions of
adult life. So in *Alice's Adventures:*

"No, no!" said the Queen. "Sentence first—verdict afterwards."

"Stuff and nonsense!" said Alice loudly. "The idea of having the sentence first!"

"Hold your tongue!" said the Queen, turning purple.

"I won't!" said Alice.

"Off with her head!" the Queen shouted at the top of her voice. Nobody moved.

"Who cares for *you*?" said Alice (she had grown to her full size by this time). "You're nothing but a pack of cards!"

At this the whole pack rose up into the air, and came flying down upon her; she gave a little scream, half of fright and half of anger, and tried to beat them off, and found herself lying on the bank, with her head in the lap of her sister, who was gently brushing away some dead leaves that had fluttered down from the trees upon her face. (96—98)

The carefully contrived order of the adult public world is a pack of cards, dead leaves on the face of a dreaming child. A clearer statement of the relative values of work and play, childhood and adulthood, would be hard to find.

In *Through the Looking-Glass*, a slightly older Alice encounters the quixotic White Knight, cheers him on his ineffectual way, and then—as a reward for kindness—becomes a rather uncertain Queen. ("Queens have to be dignified, you know!" she tells herself; "and if I really am a Queen, I shall be able to manage it quite well in time.") But soon she finds that adult life is not so simple; there are other queens lurking about. "Speak when you're spoken to!" the Red Queen tells her; and then, in a final parody of education, "You can't be a Queen, you know, till you've passed the proper examination. And the sooner we begin it, the better."

"Can you do Addition?" the White Queen asked. "What's one and one and one and one and one and one and one and one and one and one?"

"I don't know," said Alice. "I lost count."

"She can't do Addition," the Red Queen interrupted. "Can you do Subtraction? Take nine from eight."

"Nine from eight I can't, you know," Alice replied very readily: "but—"

"She can't do Subtraction," said the White Queen. "Can you do Division? Divide a loaf by a knife—what's the answer to *that?*" (193–94)

And on and on and on it goes. "What dreadful nonsense we *are* talking!" Alice says to herself. After several pages of this, the Red and White Queens fall asleep, and Alice wonders reasonably enough, "What *am* I to do?" In the final act of self-assertion that ends her nightmare, she picks up the Red Queen and exclaims, "I'll shake you into a kitten, that I will!" She awakens, of course, to find herself shaking a kitten.

The nightmares of real life are not so easily exorcised, and modern students of Alice are apt to find themselves trying to reconcile three visual images of the heroine whose exploits on behalf of the playful imagination they have been taking so seriously. The first, if they have been reading a good edition of the two books, is Tenniel's sulky Pre-Raphaelite blonde, her head too big for her body—a potent symbol. The second, if they have been lucky enough to see Carroll's series of photographs of Alice Liddell, is Alice herself at the age of seven. A bright-eyed, fearless gamin with short dark hair, she makes one doubt that she left many houses of cards standing; and one understands, as one cannot with earlier children in literature, precisely why her author thought her worthy to stand as the champion of play.

The third picture is less happy. It is a photograph Carroll took of Alice Liddell at the age of fourteen or fifteen—one of the last pictures he took of her, for he was rapidly losing interest in his onetime heroine. ("Alice seems changed a good deal, and hardly for the better—probably going through the usual awkward stage of transition," he confided to his diary a week after her thirteenth birthday [279].) The face that looks back is still imaginative and charming, but it is no longer the face of a girl who can knock down houses of cards with impunity. Alas, it is the face of a shy young Victorian woman, trapped in the world of dignified queens and respectable hostesses. It is a face that will spend the rest of its long life looking earnest. The world of work has won.

The face that we remember most happily is the second one, the actual face of Alice Liddell at the age of seven. It is this face on whose future Alice's elder sister muses at the end of *Alice's Adventures:*

> Lastly, she pictured to herself how this same little sister of hers would, in the after-time, be herself a grown woman; and how she would keep, through all her riper years, the simple and loving heart of her childhood; and how she would gather about her other little children, and make *their* eyes bright and eager with many a strange tale, perhaps even with the dream of Wonderland of long ago; and how she would feel with all their simple sorrows, and find a pleasure in all their simple joys, remembering her own child-life, and the happy summer days. (99)

A sentimental ending, certainly, and one that for all its plausibility is harder to believe in than the tale that precedes it. But the focus here is on the sister, not on Alice; and the sister, who (we have already been told) reads books without pictures, will not herself be summoning the children of the future. She is already, whatever her age, an adult, and must see the world of play through other eyes. Since to all intents and purposes the sister is Lewis Carroll himself, the ending returns us to the essential desperation of the Victorian writer who believed (how consciously is of no importance here) in the supreme value of play. Only through the use of a child protagonist could he adequately display that value; only in recounting her adventures could he grant himself the freedom to indulge in play himself—the play of language and number and symbol that raises Carroll to the status of a major English writer. But there is a fatal defect in seeing the childhood mind as the locus of the highest values in life, and it is simply that all children without exception die or grow up.

"To his coy mistress" is a literary ancestor of the Alice books, although by no obvious genealogical line. The centuries in which they appeared were too different; so were their authors. Mr. Dodgson of Christ Church could never have approved of a poem that glorified erotic sport; probably he had never read it. Yet both authors celebrated play as a supreme value, and both created protagonists who are suspicious about the wisdom of growing up. For both Alice and the reluctant mistress, adult life gives off an offensive odor. The difference is that while Alice goes on playing, the mistress refuses to play; and it makes all the difference in the world.

Carroll's own identification of growing up with death is explicit. In the poem that precedes *Through the Looking-Glass*, he summons his readers to relive Alice's childhood before it's too late:

> Come, hearken then, ere voice of dread,
>   With bitter tidings laden,
> Shall summon to unwelcome bed
>   A melancholy maiden!
> We are but older children, dear,
> Who fret to find our bedtime near.

Few beds in literature are more procreant than this one, being simultaneously a child's ordinary bed, a deathbed, and the bed to which Victorian brides let their husbands guide them as a matter of duty. In this last sense, of course, it is a later version of the same bed in which the coy mistress refuses to play.

The identification of sex with growing up is Carroll's, however, not Alice's; as a character she is presexual, and in the end she instinctively remains a player. What she sees of adult life is first sought, then found repellant for reasons that have nothing to do

36

with sexuality, whether defined as play by Marvell's century or duty by her own. She suffers neither from narcissism nor from fear; as a character she consistently holds fast to, indeed represents, play in a form that the nineteenth century could countenance. The coy mistress is very different, refusing the form of adult play that her creator has to offer. In her alluring evasiveness, she is saving herself for something better. She is one of the first Victorian heroines.

A century in which playfulness is acceptable only for children can hardly be satisfactory for those who are not earnest, and is bound to turn any adult who believes deeply in play into a pessimist and a sentimentalist. In this respect the seventeenth century was freer than the nineteenth; it allowed adults (at least fortunate adults) more latitude to play without being infantile. The coy mistress's refusal to grow up takes the form of a refusal to play which is, within the terms of the poem, deluded. Alice, a wiser character in a more foolish century, declines adulthood for precisely the opposite reason. Since our own century admires both "To His Coy Mistress" and the Alice books, we might deduce that we have the good fortune to live in a time when the playful attitude to life is licit for both children and adults. The compulsive emphasis on youthfulness for both sexes, the mechanization of games, and the loss of spontaneity throughout our whole culture suggest otherwise. Where the fear of old age and death becomes an obsession, the result is not play but paralysis, however frenetic it may look. Real adult play comes from the acceptance of death, not from the pretence that it doesn't exist. Denial of the obvious can never lead to freedom, and the orientation of Western culture today towards adolescent tastes and habits is not genuine playfulness but something quite different, which Huizinga calls Puerilism.

There are probably more mistresses and less coyness in the world than ever before, but activity whose ulterior purpose is to persuade the actors that they are alive, young, and wanted is deadly serious. In Sennett's words:

As belief in the public domain has come to an end, the erosion of a sense of self-distance, and thus the difficulty of playing in adult life, has taken one more step. But it is an important step. A person cannot imagine playing with his environment, playing with the facts of his position in society, playing with his appearances to others, because these conditions are now part and parcel of himself.[7]

The late twentieth century has completed the nineteenth century's transformation of sex from play into work, as contemporary medicine, sociology, and literature plentifully attest. Since sex has always been fundamental to adult forms of play, it is now hard to identify any forms of grown-up activity that bear the genuine birthmark of *Homo ludens*. When we do find them, we may expect them to be hidden safely behind the mask of earnestness and work. Hide-and-seek is the most enduring game in life and literature, and what other hiding place is left?

3. Home and Away

T HE HIGHEST COMPLIMENT a children's book can receive is for
critics to say that it isn't for children at all. When adults annex
a book like *Alice's Adventures in Wonderland* or *Huckleberry Finn* for
themselves, it achieves a higher literary status even than that of
being numbered among the "classic" works for children, works
such as *Now We Are Six, Treasure Island,* or—a more complicated
case, as we shall see—*The Wind in the Willows.*

The criteria by which a book may be placed in one category or
the other have been much discussed but never clearly defined,
and they are a great deal less obvious than they may seem. To say
that a book appeals to people of many different ages is no help
here; all the books I have listed do that, as do *The Iliad, Old Pos-
sum's Book of Practical Cats, Gulliver's Travels,* and most books about
the Civil War. Nor is it enough to identify the primary audience
that the writer had in mind, since *Huckleberry Finn* and the Alice
books were written, illustrated, and marketed for children. Realism is no criterion; most fiction for adults is no more realistic
than most children's fiction. That a book raises issues which are
intellectually beyond the comprehension of most children may
seem a slightly more promising standard; yet how many adults
are equipped to comprehend the linguistic and logical issues in
Through the Looking-Glass, the moral issues in *Huckleberry Finn,* or
indeed the full range of questions raised by any profound work of

literature? That many adults understand more of these things than many children is hardly a basis for confident taxonomizing.

It is improbable that any single standard can be used to tell us which of the books we deeply admire are "really" children's books, which are adult books (a phrase with contemporary connotations that imply sexual interest as a criterion), and which are genuinely ambiguous. The books we *don't* deeply admire may present fewer problems, but then the question of their status is correspondingly less interesting.

This essay will speculate on why some books fall into one category, some into another. My intrinsic approach will not, admittedly, apply to all works of fiction, but where it does apply it should almost infallibly distinguish books that are genuinely for children. It applies strikingly to two of the works cited above, *Huckleberry Finn* and *The Wind in the Willows*, about which Grahame's biographer had this to say:

> It is interesting to compare the double theme which preoccupies Grahame in *The Wind in the Willows*—the judgment of Innocence on the World, the deep basic symbolism of the River—with the somewhat different treatment both receive in Mark Twain's *Huckleberry Finn*. Twain's classic had appeared in 1885, and there is little doubt that Grahame knew it well. He certainly gave a copy to his son.[1]

Twain's influence on Grahame's book is palpable, not so much in the use both make of the River as in the tall tales and female disguise by which Toad escapes from a series of captors. Both are stories of escape and return, of naive innocence ambiguously overcoming the perils of the Wide World, of civilization making ominous advances into the heartland of natural goodness. Each ends with the protagonist and his friends restored to honor and fortune. Yet nearly everyone will agree that Grahame has written a genuine children's book and Twain has not. Why?

I believe that a key to what appeals to children in Grahame's book is this: in *The Wind in the Willows,* the major escape (Toad's) is from prison to home. Although several of the characters are tempted by travel, home is clearly where the characters belong and where, after many vicissitudes, they return. As Mole feels when he has found again the home he left on a spring morning:

> He saw clearly how plain and simple—how narrow, even—it all was; but clearly, too, how much it all meant to him, and the special value of some such anchorage in one's existence. He did not at all want to abandon the new life and its splendid spaces. . . . But it was good to think he had this to come back to, this place which was all his own, these things which were so glad to see him again and could always be counted upon for the same simple welcome.[2]

For the River-bankers, as for Dorothy in *The Wizard of Oz,* there is no place like home; and while that attitude may not in real life be any more characteristic of children than of adults, it is certainly common in children's books. In *Huckleberry Finn,* on the contrary, the escape is *from* home, and it is never repented of or shown to be mistaken, although it is not altogether successful. Home, for Huck and his author, is the problem, not the solution. Huck says in the beginning: "The Widow Douglas, she took me for her son, and allowed she would sivilize me; but it was rough living in the house all the time, considering how dismal regular and decent the widow was in all her ways; and so when I couldn't stand it no longer, I lit out. I got into my old rags, and my sugar-hogshead again, and was free and satisfied."[3] Returning to the Widow's makes Huck feel "so lonesome I most wished I was dead" (9). At the end of the book, returned home once more, he hasn't changed his mind and is on the brink of another escape: "But I reckon I got to light out for the Territory ahead of the rest, because Aunt Sally she's going to adopt me and sivilize me and I can't stand it. I been there before" (229).

For Huck, home is the place where, when you have to go there, you almost wish you were dead. In contrast to home, there is the raft, symbol of random motion and effortless escape. "We said there warn't no home like a raft, after all. Other places do seem so cramped up and smothery, but a raft don't. You feel mighty free and easy and comfortable on a raft" (96).

When home is a privileged place, exempt from the most serious problems of life and civilization—when staying (or returning) home is something like an absolute moral value—we are probably dealing with a story for children. When home is the chief place from which we must escape, either to grow up or (as in Huck's case) to remain innocent, then we are involved in a story for adolescents or adults. As Geraldine D. Poss says of an earlier Grahame children's story, "The world which [the characters] envision is one which simply ignores death, women, and pressure to achieve," a statement which might with almost equal justice be made about *The Wind in the Willows*.[4] It is precisely "death, women, and pressure to achieve" that Huck Finn tries to escape by leaving home. Grahame's characters, however, live in a place that gives them few reasons for escape, a fact which inevitably leads some critics to the suspicion that their author has done their escaping for them. Thus common opinion is correct: *The Wind in the Willows* is a children's book and *Huckleberry Finn* is not.[5]

Viewed in this light, the ancestor of all journey books, *The Odyssey*, is an instructive mixture. Ithaca after the Trojan War is in many ways far from being a privileged place, yet Odysseus' aim throughout the poem is to return there, and he is clearly right to do so. In his ten-year journey home from Troy, he encounters enough picturesque monsters and boys'-own adventures to furnish a shelf of children's books. The modesty of his goals and his success in achieving them make Odysseus unique among epic heroes, and in modern times *The Odyssey* has almost certainly been read by more children (and more often adapted for young readers) than any other epic. Later writers, however, have frequently found its ending disappointingly tame and have transformed

Odysseus into an emblem of the proto-modern, searching mind by taking him in late middle age permanently away from Ithaca. Hence the sequels by Dante, Tennyson, Kazantzakis. The final escape is not from monsters or suitors but from a safe domesticity.

Escape is one of the most thoughtlessly used words in the critical vocabulary, particularly when coupled with the phrase *from reality*, and in analyzing stories that either narrate escapes or are alleged to be escapist, we need to be careful about what we mean. In defending fairy stories and other forms of fantasy against the negative connotations of the word, J. R. R. Tolkien provides us with the beginnings of a useful distinction:

> In what the misusers are fond of calling Real Life, Escape is evidently as a rule very practical, and may even be heroic. In real life it is difficult to blame it, unless it fails; in criticism it would seem to be the worse the better it succeeds. . . . Why should a man be scorned if, finding himself in prison, he tries to get out and go home? Or if, when he cannot do so, he thinks and talks about other topics than jailers and prison-walls? The world outside has not become less real because the prisoner cannot see it. In using Escape in this way the critics have chosen the wrong word, and, what is more, they are confusing, not always by sincere error, the Escape of the Prisoner with the Flight of the Deserter.[6]

To escape means simply to get away from something unpleasant; both unmerited imprisonment and duty may be unpleasant, but our moral judgment of the escaper will depend largely upon which of these categories of experience he is escaping. In *Huckleberry Finn*, almost no readers will judge Jim unfavorably for escaping from slavery, just as in *The Wind in the Willows* Toad's escape from prison is clearly the right course of action for him to take. Whether Huck is quite so justified in escaping from religion, education, manners, and clothes into what can be only a temporary idyll is more debatable; those moralists who believe in good citizenship, strong families, and the work ethic will certainly say no.

It is when we try to decide whether whole books and their authors are escapist, however, that the question becomes really complicated. With what view of reality and the consequences of action is an author required to present his audience of children or adults? If he believes, as both Twain and Grahame did, that full participation in the adult, civilized world is a form of imprisonment, is he required to show his characters accepting such participation as their duty, or may he allow them to attempt what ever forms of escape seem most practicable to them? And if they try the second alternative, must their author show them failing? Twain did so and is regarded as a realist, despite the fact that Huck begins and ends the story independently wealthy and Jim is freed by the providential death of his owner. Grahame chose instead to create an environment which is substantially free from the pressures of adult civilization—although those pressures are certainly felt in the story—and at the end of their adventures, his characters are as safe and happy as they were at the beginning, having learned anew to reject the Wide World of manmade laws, motor-cars, and jails. We are probably safe in assuming that middle-class life along the Fowey River circa 1908 was in actuality pleasanter than frontier life on the banks of the Mississippi in the 1840s; we have no warrant for concluding that Grahame's book is more escapist, in the negative sense of the word, than Twain's. If modern civilization is a moral disaster, then getting away from it (by staying home, in the case of a children's book) is a duty in both life and literature, so long as we are clear about our reasons for rejecting it.

REGARDLESS of whether home is benign or terrible, of course, people do like to get away sometimes, and Grahame's characters are no exception. *The Wind in the Willows* is the story of their varying attempts at adventure and of the lessons they learn about home and escape. The book begins when Mole, fed up with spring cleaning, ventures out of his hole and discovers the river.

"Something up above was calling him imperiously" (2), and in answering the call he soon finds himself sharing Rat's broader and more sociable way of life. Indeed, it looks for a while as though Mole's new life will represent a genuine break with the past, for he shows such signs of venturesomeness that Rat, the wisest of all the characters, feels compelled to warn him against the world that lies beyond the horizon.

> "Beyond the Wild Wood comes the Wide World," said the Rat. "And that's something that doesn't matter, either to you or me. I've never been there, and I'm never going, nor you either, if you've got any sense at all. Don't ever refer to it again, please." (14)

Leaving home is all right only if one doesn't go too far, or for too long. Neither Rat nor Mole ever ventures into the Wide World; that act of folly is left to the most foolish of all the characters, with dire results. When Mole goes even so far as the Wild Wood, he finds it a place of fear and menace after his rescue, and he recognizes that he has been taught a lesson he will never again forget:

> The Mole saw clearly that he was an animal of tilled field and hedgerow, linked to the ploughed furrow, the frequented pasture, the lane of evening lingerings, the cultivated garden-plot. . . . he must be wise, must keep to the pleasant places in which his lines were laid and which held adventure enough, in their way, to last for a lifetime. (101)

It is after the Wild Wood that he begins to miss his hole, to search for it with much difficulty, and to appreciate it more than ever when he has found it again.

The Rat is a much more adventurous animal as well as a more experienced one, and his reluctance to travel widely cannot be due to either ignorance or timidity. As he has warned Mole against the Wide World, so he warns the footloose Toad against wandering about in a gipsy caravan, a warning which events jus-

45

tify when Toad, after a nearly fatal encounter with a motor-car, falls in love with mechanical transport. That the car is the chief symbol—a negative one—of the modern world in Grahame's book is appropriate, since it represents both rapid travel and industrialization. Rat is so consistently wise throughout the book that it comes as a major surprise when he too is tempted with the wanderlust against which he has all along warned. The agents of temptation are swallows preparing to migrate south. "With closed eyes he dared to dream a moment in full abandonment, and when he looked again the river seemed steely and chill, the green fields grey and lifeless. Then his loyal heart seemed to cry out on his weaker self for its treachery" (210–11).

The vocabulary makes it clear that for Rat to leave like the birds would be the flight of the deserter, an evasion of responsibility, and a denial of what he knows about life. Having overcome temptation, however, he is almost immediately plunged into a hypnotic state by the yarns of the Sea Rat, a true escapist if ever there was, who has much to say about the glories of Sicily and Constantinople.

> Mechanically he returned home, gathered together a few small necessaries and special treasures he was fond of, and put them in a satchel; acting with slow deliberation, moving about the room like a sleep-walker; listening ever with parted lips. He swung the satchel over his shoulder, carefully selected a stout stick for his wayfaring, and with no haste, but with no hesitation at all, he stepped across the threshold just as the Mole appeared at the door. (229–30)

This time Mole, determined teacher of a lesson he himself had learned only recently, returns the favor and prevents the folly of an escape from home. That roaming the world is such a temptation, even for the less flighty characters, demonstrates beyond doubt that the virtues of home are a lesson of experience, not merely an instinct of the fearful. Huck Finn's preparations before he departs from the "home" where Pap is holding him prisoner are told in quite a different tone:

I took the sack of corn meal and took it to where the canoe was hid, and shoved the vines and branches apart and put it in; then I done the same with the side of bacon; then the whisky jug; I took all the coffee and sugar there was, and all the ammunition; I took the wadding; I took the bucket and gourd, I took a dipper and a tin cup, and my old saw and two blankets, and the skillet and the coffee-pot. I took fishlines and matches and other things—everything that was worth a cent. I cleaned out the place. . . . I fetched out the gun, and now I was done. (30–31)

The contrast between two attitudes towards home, and two kinds of escape, could hardly be better illustrated.

Of the major characters in *The Wind in the Willows*, it is only Toad who for any considerable length of time sets home at naught and gives way to the temptations of distance. We should remember that properly speaking, he is Mister Toad of Toad Hall, an Edwardian landed gentleman, and that as a gentleman he naturally possesses a confidence (unwarranted, of course) in his ability to make the inhabitants of the Wide World do his bidding; this confidence is entirely unshared by any other character in the story. Among other things, *The Wind in the Willows* is a satire on Toad's belief that traditional social distinctions count for much in the alien world of twentieth-century human civilization. (In Twain's world he might be a Grangerford.) It is not until Toad finds himself described in the courtroom as an "incorrigible rogue and hardened ruffian" (149–50)—all he has done, after all, is to "borrow" a motor-car—that he begins to understand the virtues of home. His escape involves the humiliation of dressing up as a washerwoman, and since he has forgotten to remove his wallet from the abandoned garments of his true rank, he undergoes a salutary education in the life of poverty before reaching the sanctuary of Rat's home. He is even tossed into a canal by a woman of plebeian habits (243).

Once he reaches the riverbank, a further shock awaits him: Toad Hall is in the hands of invading stoats and weasels. At this point (though not for the first or the last time), Toad is properly repentant of his past and puts himself in the hands of his friends, Rat, Badger, and Mole. By use of an underground passage into Toad Hall that only Badger knows about (Toad's ignorance embraces not only the Wide World but even his own house), the heroes overcome the occupying forces, and Toad Hall is liberated. Henceforth Toad will abide more humbly and wisely at home— or so his friends hope.

The price of Toad's travels, then, is to have to fight for his home when he returns. Appropriately, the final chapter of *The Wind in the Willows* is entitled "The Return of Ulysses." The benign littoral enclave is not a free gift of the gods; like Ithaca, it needs to be guarded with wisdom, discretion, and sometimes force. Toad's escape from home (the flight of the deserter) makes necessary the far more desperate flight back (the escape of the prisoner), as well as the battle that follows. The second escape is, of course, implausibly easy; merely breaking jail and returning home does not normally guarantee immunity from the law. But the lessons of the adventure are plain—if not to Toad, at least to the reader.

WHAT, BY WAY OF EPILOGUE, about J. R. R. Tolkien? In *The Hobbit,* his early children's book, Tolkien created a race of beings who, in the felicity of their surroundings, their preference for living in holes, and their reluctance to seek adventures in the wider world, are recognizably indebted to *The Wind in the Willows.* [7] Bilbo Baggins, whose attachment to home is similar to Rat's, is prevailed upon by the wizard Gandalf to take part in a quest so that he may learn about the dangers of the outside world. Those who will not inform themselves about evil, Tolkien seems to be saying, are likely to have no defense against it when they find themselves forced to protect their homes. Bilbo's quest is successful, both in its immediate object and as a device for educating him, but it is significant that the only reward he seeks is to be allowed to return home. This wish is repeated throughout the book as a sort of refrain. Once returned, he finds that his house and effects are in the process of being sold at auction, and his repossession of home, though not as arduous as Toad's, costs him considerable bother. At the end of the book, however, he has returned to a well-earned domesticity, interrupted only by occasional visits to the Elves. There is no indication that he will ever again trade the placid virtues of home for the more speculative benefits of adventure. Even the great ring of power has come to serve the domestic purpose of helping him avoid unwelcome callers. The lessons he has learned do not qualify his attachment to home; rather, they equip him to defend his island of peace against an increasingly threatening world outside.

Lord of the Rings, which is generally agreed not to be a children's book, comes to rather different conclusions. Frodo Baggins, his two cousins, and his servant Sam set out with a reluctance equal to Bilbo's on a far longer and more dangerous quest. "The wide world is all about you," an Elf reminds them early in their adventures: "you can fence yourselves in, but you cannot for ever fence it out." [8] This advice proves to be one of the chief lessons of the story. On their return, Frodo and his companions find the Shire occupied by the very forces of evil they have helped to vanquish in the world outside—the hobbits who stayed home not having learned the lessons of defense—and although the invaders are quickly put to flight, Frodo finds it impossible to settle back into domestic life. After the pain and temptations he has experienced, only the wisdom and healing power of the Elves can make him whole. The Shire, for all its virtues, is simply too narrow a place after what he has learned and undergone. Frodo has outgrown his home, and he commits a more elegant equivalent of lighting out for the Territory. Setting out with Bilbo (who is not at all the home-loving character he was in *The Hobbit*) and the lords of the Elves for the Grey Havens, he tries to explain himself to the uncomprehending Sam:

> "But," said Sam, and tears started in his eyes, "I thought you were going to enjoy the Shire, too, for years and years, after all you have done."
>
> "So I thought too, once. But I have been too deeply hurt, Sam. I

tried to save the Shire, and it has been saved, but not for me. It must often be so, Sam, when things are in danger: some one has to give them up, lose them, so that others may keep them. . . . You will be the Mayor, of course, as long as you want to be, and the most famous gardener in history; and you will read things out of the Red Book, and keep alive the memory of the age that is gone, so that people will remember the Great Danger and so love their beloved land all the more. And that will keep you as busy and as happy as anyone can be, as long as your part of the Story goes on.

"Come now, ride with me!"[9]

"Come now, ride with me!"—these are Frodo's last words, and in this context at least, they could not be the last words of the main character in a children's book. The Escape of the Prisoner has taken on a dimension that transcends the distinction between home and the wide world. It is Sam, however, the boy hero who never grows up,[10] protagonist of a thousand stories of adventure for children, who pronounces the book's final sentence when he returns home at nightfall: "Well, I'm back."

4. Sherlock Holmes, Order, and the Late-Victorian Mind

F EW CHARACTERS in all of literature are as widely known as Sherlock Holmes. From his first appearance in *A Study in Scarlet* (1887), the four novels and fifty-six short stories of which he is the protagonist have been among the most continuously popular works of fiction ever created. Even among those who have never read any of the stories or seen the film and television adaptations, there must be very few people over the age of ten in the English-speaking world who have never heard of Sherlock Holmes, or of his equally imaginary chronicler, Dr. Watson. As T. S. Eliot pointed out in the *Criterion* in 1929, Holmes is *real* in a way that only the greatest fictional characters ever achieve. Less sophisticated readers think so, too: letters of admiration and requests for help are still addressed to the mythical rooms of a man who, had he ever lived at all, would now be a hundred and thirty years old. No other Victorian literary character, not even Alice, has maintained so powerful a hold on so many twentieth-century readers' imaginations.

Holmes's continued popularity with all levels of readers is all the more striking when one reflects that he is probably the most cerebral protagonist of any importance in English fiction. His life is almost wholly intellectual. "I am a brain, Watson," he says in

"The Mazarin Stone." "The rest of me is a mere appendix" (II, 1014). [1] When he has no case to occupy his mind, he often takes morphine or cocaine because he cannot bear the boredom of everyday life. He has no friends but Watson, he says in "The Five Orange Pips." He is jarringly egotistical. His contempt for the average mind—usually represented by poor Watson's—is displayed again and again. "There, Watson!" he announces after a successful series of deductions in *The Valley of Fear.* "What do you think of pure reason and its fruit?" (II, 773). To that commitment he is rarely unfaithful. He never once falls in love. "All emotions, and that one particularly," we learn in "A Scandal in Bohemia," the first of the short stories, "were abhorrent to his cold, precise but admirably balanced mind. He was, I take it, the most perfect reasoning and observing machine that the world has seen. . . . He never spoke of the softer passions, save with a gibe and a sneer" (I, 161).

Although a gentleman by birth and education, he belongs to no club, unlike Watson. He is, in fact, the sort of isolated intellectual who today would be called alienated: introverted, frighteningly analytical, and often cynical. In at least one case, "The Yellow Face," his cynicism leads him to the wrong conclusion. Although patriotic, he has little use for the conventions, in some cases even the laws, of Victorian society that it is his profession to uphold. He entirely lacks the glamour of James Bond, the snob appeal of Lord Peter Wimsey, the ostentatious whimsicality of Nero Wolfe.

This is hardly a recipe for a hero of popular fiction. Yet Holmes, accompanied and interpreted by his more conventional friend, has been so much in demand for over ninety years that his creator reluctantly abandoned all thought of killing him off, and other authors continue to write nostalgic best-sellers about him today. He has also been the subject of the most tedious pseudoscholarship in the history of letters, most of it premised on the facetious assumption that Holmes was a historical character whose biography needs filling in. Meanwhile his most important fictional predecessors, Poe's Dupin and Gaboriau's Lecoq, have faded into relative obscurity.

Holmes's real status as an anomalously popular hero of fiction has rarely been examined by historians of literature or ideas. Whether because of its ambiguous standing somewhere in the no-man's-land between "popular culture" and serious literature, or because the people who write articles about what university Holmes attended and whether he was ever an actor have driven everyone else away, there has been remarkably little critical discussion of the Holmes canon. Yet it amply repays study. Conan Doyle published stories about Sherlock Holmes over a period of forty years, from 1887 to 1927; the range of life—of people, settings, ideas—that Holmes encounters or reflects upon in that time is extraordinarily wide. For reasons I will discuss presently, the stories written after 1914 (all but one of them set before the war) are inferior to the earlier ones, and any high literary claims must rest on *The Hound of the Baskervilles* and a dozen or so short stories. Nevertheless, the canon as a whole, with its observant, analytical hero who comes into professional contact with all strata of urban and rural society from kings (for example, in "A Scandal in Bohemia") to beggars (for example, in "The Man with the Twisted Lip"), offers an unrivalled and largely overlooked source for the study of ideas, attitudes, and culture in the period when British power and confidence were at their peak, from Queen Victoria's golden jubilee until the outbreak of the First World War.

As Thomas Love Peacock pointed out in "An Essay on Fashionable Literature," "The moral and political character of the age or nation may be read by an attentive observer even in its lightest literature, how remote soever *prima facie* from morals and politics." [2] The minds of authors and characters are revealed not only by what they assert but also by what they take for granted. When the author writes for and is popular with a wide audience, attentive readers at a later time may learn something about what views of itself and its world that audience was prepared to accept. Furthermore, of all forms of "light literature," the detective story is the most inescapably concerned with moral issues. A crime is committed; the criminal must be discovered and judged. The opportunities detective fiction offers for the study of changing ideas about the motives and consequences of human action will be obvious.

THE PATTERN of intellect at war with mystery is set at the very beginning, in *A Study in Scarlet,* and although it is developed in subsequent works, it never changes in any essential way. In view of the notorious inconsistencies of biographical detail from one Holmes story to another, this coherence of purpose over a period of forty years needs to be stressed. Deduction, the elucidation of mysteries through scientific reason, is Holmes's ruling passion, and only by subordinating everything else to it can he serve as the guardian of a threatened society that his author means him to be. If as a result he seems somewhat one-dimensional as a character, that is an essential part of the stories' meaning.

Holmes is first described by Stamford, a medical friend of Watson's, in terms that would be equally apt at the end of Holmes's career:

> "It is not easy to express the inexpressible," he answered with a laugh. "Holmes is a little too scientific for my tastes—it approaches to cold-bloodedness. I could imagine his giving a friend a little pinch of the latest vegetable alkaloid, not out of malevolence, you understand, but simply out of a spirit of inquiry in order to have an accurate idea of the effects. To do him justice, I think that he would take it himself with the same readiness. He appears to have a passion for definite and exact knowledge." (I, 17)

Stamford's only purpose in the story is to introduce Holmes and Watson; having accomplished this momentous act, he disappears forever. At the moment of the introduction, Holmes—as vivid and fully realized as he will ever be—has just discovered an infallible test for distinguishing blood from all other stains. One of the two most famous lines in the whole cycle follows when, glancing at Watson, Holmes declares, "You have been in Afghanistan, I perceive" (I, 18). It is a powerful entrance, and although we learn about the darker side of his nature later on, it defines Holmes as a character forever.

Fittingly, the second chapter of *A Study in Scarlet* is entitled "The Science of Deduction." It is here that Watson, a slow learner but no fool, begins to grasp the dimensions of the man with whom he has so rashly committed himself to share rooms. At first he is baffled. In both qualities and habits, Holmes is unlike anyone Watson has ever met. He is alternately energetic and lethargic. He seems to have no profession, yet his activities appear to be guided by a purpose.

> He was not studying medicine. . . . Neither did he appear to have pursued any course of reading which might fit him for a degree in science or any other recognized portal which would give him an entrance into the learned world. Yet his zeal for certain studies was remarkable, and within eccentric limits his knowledge was so extraordinarily ample and minute that his observations have fairly astounded me. Surely no man would work so hard or attain such precise information unless he had some definite end in view. (I, 20)

A methodical observer himself, Watson makes up a list which he heads "Sherlock Holmes—his limits." It is not much help. Next to Knowledge of Literature, Philosophy, and Astronomy, Watson writes "Nil." Knowledge of Politics is "Feeble," of Botany "Variable": Holmes knows a great deal about poisons but nothing of gardening. Geology is "Practical, but limited"; Holmes can tell different soils at a glance and explain where each one came from. His knowledge of chemistry is "Profound"; anatomy, "Accurate, but unsystematic"; sensational literature, "Immense." He plays the violin well, is an expert in the arts of self-defense, and has "a good practical knowledge of British law" (I, 21–22). Having completed this odd list, Watson throws it into the fire in despair.

It is Watson's deprecation of Holmes's magazine article "The Book of Life" that leads to enlightenment of a sort, for in defending his article Holmes reveals his profession. The article falls into the nineteenth-century tradition of essays applying scientific canons of reason and evidence to everyday life. What is quoted of it suggests the influence of Thomas Henry Huxley, a writer whom Conan Doyle greatly admired:

> From a drop of water, a logician could infer the possibility of an Atlantic or a Niagara without having seen or heard of one or the other. So all life is a great chain, the nature of which is known whenever we are shown a single link of it. Like all other arts, the Science of Deduction and Analysis is one which can only be acquired by long and patient study. . . .

The man whose knowledge of philosophy was "Nil" proves to have a philosophical bent after all. (His knowledge of literature and politics will similarly expand in later stories.) It is, however, applied largely to the needs of Holmes's own profession. In a sentence that we will see illustrated time and again in this and later stories, the article declares, "By a man's finger-nails, by his coat-sleeve, by his boots, by his trouser-knees, by the callosities of his forefinger and thumb, by his expression, by his shirt-cuffs—by each of these things a man's calling is plainly revealed" (I, 23). Through proper observation and analysis, the scientific mind can make deductions in everyday life that will strike less acute witnesses as magical.

The particular pattern of scientific reasoning that Holmes finds most useful is akin to that of the archeologist or evolutionary biologist and involves working back from effects to causes. After demonstrating for the first time the success of his methods, he provides a further explanation of them at the end of *A Study in Scarlet:*

> Most people, if you describe a train of events to them, will tell you what the result would be. They can put those events together in their minds, and argue from them that something will come to pass. There are few people, however, who, if you told them a result, would be able to evolve from their own inner consciousness what the steps were which led up to that result. This power is what I mean when I talk of reasoning backward, or analytically. (I, 83–84)

He expands on this explanation in "The Five Orange Pips," when he declares, "As Cuvier could correctly describe a whole animal by the contemplation of a single bone, so the observer who has thoroughly understood one link in a series of incidents should be able to accurately state all the other ones, both before and after" (I, 225). It is this kind of anterior reconstruction that Holmes manages to accomplish in case after case.

Whether Holmes's methods and results in his detecting career really satisfy scientific standards of rigor is another question entirely. It has often been pointed out that many of his deductions are far from airtight. Although he frequently denounces guesswork, at times he seems alarmingly dependent on lucky intuitions. In one case, "The Musgrave Ritual," his solution depends on the assumption that an elm and an oak have not grown at all in two hundred and fifty years; but then, we have already been told that his knowledge of botany is variable. It would be possible to pick many holes in both his methods and his conclusions. The important point, however, is that he is conceived—and conceives of himself—as a man who applies scientific methods to the detection of crime, and that his success as a detective is due to those methods. He uses them more convincingly than most other fictional detectives, and he hews to them with a religious intensity. His reaction to Watson's first account of his exploits is not merely

in character but deeply revealing: "Honestly, I cannot congratulate you upon it. Detection is, or ought to be, an exact science and
should be treated in the same cold and unemotional manner. You
have attempted to tinge it with romanticism, which produces
much the same effect as if you worked a love-story or an elope-
ment into the fifth proposition of Euclid" (I, 90). Like many other
nineteenth-century enthusiasts, Holmes thinks of science as a
purifying discipline whose chief goal is the clearing away of mysteries. The difference lies in the particular mysteries to which he
applies it—and, perhaps, in the utter single-mindedness with
which he devotes himself to his vocation. Tennyson's King Arthur
was not the only kind of Victorian protagonist who represented
"soul at war with sense."

Anyone who carries reason this far is bound to be rather solitary. In the second novel, *The Sign of Four* (1890), from which the
above passage is quoted, we begin to see some of the sacrifices
that Holmes has made in the pursuit of detachment, for it is in this
story that Watson finds a wife. After what we have come to recognize as a typically brilliant series of deductions, Holmes is told
of his collaborator's impending defection from Baker Street. "I
feared as much," he responds. "I really cannot congratulate you."
When Watson wishes to know whether he disapproves of the
young woman, Holmes declares that, on the contrary, she is brilliant and charming. "But love is an emotional thing," he adds,
"and whatever is emotional is opposed to that true cold reason
which I place above all things. I should never marry myself, lest I
bias my judgment" (I, 157). The price of his commitment is lifelong isolation and loneliness, and while these states are frequently mitigated by Watson himself (whose wife soon disappears) and by success and fame, they never cease to be the essential conditions of Holmes's existence. At the end of *The Sign of
Four*, fame is in the future and Watson is about to disappear.
Credit for the case having gone to the police, Watson wonders
"what remains for you?" The answer, which ends the novel, is

genuinely tragic: " 'For me,' said Sherlock Holmes, 'there still remains the cocaine-bottle.' And he stretched his long white hand up for it" (I, 158).

WHAT WAS it all *for*, we might well ask at this point? Why such dedication, such an apparatus of self-conscious methodology, and above all such sacrifices, merely to be a private detective? The answer lies in some Victorian attitudes towards crime, mystery, and their detection. When we have explored these attitudes and Holmes's relation to them, we may be in a better position to understand his resonance as a literary character.

Much Victorian literature makes it clear that for the comfortable classes in nineteenth-century England, crime and revolution were related concepts. Both were threats to the social order, and many people did not distinguish closely between them. For a variety of reasons—the growth of poverty and social unrest that followed the industrial revolution, the example of repeated revolutions on the Continent (Tennyson's "red fool-fury of the Seine"), the rise of socialism and of labor unions, the dependence of affluent households on servants whose loyalty might be questionable—those whose interests lay in the existing social order felt threatened and vulnerable throughout virtually the whole nineteenth century. Naturally they demanded protection.

Speaking of the mid-Victorian police, Geoffrey Best maintains: "I cannot rid myself of the impression that its main function was the protection of the property, the amenities and the institutions of the propertied: their homes and business premises, their parks and promenades, their religion and their politics. These good things badly needed protection."[3] Although the middle and upper classes' sense of being a besieged minority eased somewhat in the second half of the century, it did not disappear either in country or in city. The country squire or West End gentleman who feels himself inadequately protected against reds, foreign agitators, unionized laborers, or simply vagrants is a figure of fun

59

when he turns up in the plays of Shaw, but he had many real counterparts in the days when Sherlock Holmes began plying his trade. Any serious crime was a threat. An unsolved crime might be a mortal threat, for it left an unknown enemy at large, perhaps in one's own house. "The butler did it" was a revealing fear before it was a joke. The two nations' ominous predilection for masquerading as each other (for example, in "The Man with the Twisted Lip," one of the most satirical of the stories) made things even more ambiguous.

The crimes Holmes encounters include not only murder, the staple of later detective fiction, but blackmail of the rich and famous (for example, in "Charles Augustus Milverton"); theft on a grand scale, frequently from the aristocracy or from major institutions such as banks ("The Red-Headed League"); attempts to inherit property and position illicitly (*The Hound of the Baskervilles*); revenge for crimes committed in the conquest of the Empire (*The Sign of Four*); a reign of terror by a corrupt labor union (*The Valley of Fear*); crimes whose roots lie in radical political agitation ("The Red Circle"); and espionage that threatens the security of Britain itself ("The Naval Treaty," "The Second Stain," "The Bruce-Partington Plans," "His Last Bow"). Three of the four novels involve secret societies, a focus of much late-Victorian and Edwardian paranoia.[4] The importance of these crimes is greater than that of the individuals who commit them or are their immediate victims. In solving them, Holmes does more than simply satisfy his clients or uphold the abstractions of the law. He single-handedly defends an entire social order whose relatively fortunate members feel it to be deeply threatened by forces that only he is capable of overcoming. "I am," he says in *The Sign of Four*, "the last and highest court of appeal in detection" (I, 90). When all else has failed—and the police almost always fail in the earlier Holmes stories—the isolated, disclassed genius is the one who saves the day. No wonder that by the end of the cycle he has numbered among his clients Queen Victoria, King Edward VII, the pope, the king of Bohemia, the king of Scandinavia, the royal house of Holland, the sultan, and more than one British prime minister.

"The values put forward by the detective story from the time of Holmes to the beginning of World War II," Julian Symons observes in his excellent history of the form, ". . . are those of a class in society that felt it had everything to lose by social change."[5] This generalization applies most obviously to the detective fiction of the 1920s and 1930s, in which the detective is frequently an aristocrat and the whole effect is often deliberately snobbish and reactionary. Dorothy Sayers' Lord Peter Wimsey, Margery Allingham's Albert Campion, and Ngaio Marsh's Roderick Alleyn clearly fit this mold. The Holmes stories, on the contrary, subject the English class system to as penetrating a scrutiny as it ever received from Jane Austen or Charles Dickens, and Holmes himself frequently shows contempt for his aristocratic or royal clients. It would be most accurate to say, however, that the world of the Holmes stories is merely a more realistic one, in which aristocrats are comparatively rare and the majority of crimes do not take place on country-house weekends. The conventions of the detective story as Conan Doyle found and formed them in the 1880s and 1890s were far less rigid and escapist than they became in the hands of his successors. Perhaps one reason was that before 1914 there was less nostalgia (among both writers and readers) for a fading England where everyone knew his place and the upper class maintained its perquisites intact.

Whatever the reasons, the greater realism and more jaundiced view of wealth and power in the Holmes stories should not blind us to the fact that their essential conservatism is not altogether different from that of later detective fiction. Order, if not always law, is upheld, and in those cases where Holmes allows the criminal to escape, it is either because the victim represented a greater threat to society than the criminal (as in "Charles Augustus Milverton") or because the crime was a pardonable act of revenge for acts that the law is helpless to redress ("The Crooked Man"). The law, after all, is a weak reed in the Holmes stories; society needs more effective protection. As Symons continues:

> On the social level, then, what crime literature offered to its readers for half a century from 1890 onward was a reassuring world in which those who tried to disturb the established order were always discovered and punished. Society's agent, the detective, was the single character allowed to have high intellectual attainments. He might be by ordinary standards (that is, those of his readers) eccentric, quaint, apparently a bit silly, but his knowledge was always great, and in practice he was omniscient. . . . Part of Holmes's attraction was that, far more than any of his later rivals, he was so evidently a Nietzschean superior man. It was comforting to have such a man on one's side.[6]

It is not quite accurate to say that the detective was the only character with "high intellectual attainments." There was also the master criminal, whose archetype in detective fiction is the brilliant Professor Moriarty, with whom Holmes grapples at the edge of the Reichenbach Falls. "He is the Napoleon of crime, Watson," Holmes explains in "The Final Problem." "He is the organizer of half that is evil and of nearly all that is undetected in this great city. He is a genius, a philosopher, an abstract thinker" (I, 471). It takes no great discernment to observe that Moriarty is Holmes's mirror opposite—fittingly, we are led to believe that they died grasped in each other's embrace, as though a single character had been divided and rejoined—and that in the face of such a dire threat to society, the police are wholly ineffectual.

Readers of the stories seldom ask themselves why the police should be such buffoons when confronted by an intelligent criminal. Such fumbling helplessness of course became one of the conventions of a rigidly conventional literary form, but a convention, at least while it is forming, generally reveals an attitude. I have already pointed out that the prestige of the police was low when Doyle began to write, and this historical fact has something to do with the popularity of an unofficial genius like Holmes. But we might also extend Symons' point about the detective's permitted eccentricity by saying that the detective's success is in considerable measure dependent on that eccentricity. The police are conventional not merely in the literary but also in the social sense of the word; they think and operate by conventions. As a result, they are often the victims of their own orthodoxy, of their social roles as respectable, practical, untheoretical men, whenever they encounter an especially bright or unorthodox criminal. They become blinded by their own unimaginative assumptions about how people act, which are those of the classes they are sworn to protect. No policeman is likely to deduce that a long-lost heir to a baronetcy will set himself up in the neighborhood under an assumed identity and train a gigantic hound to frighten the superstitious baronet to death, or that a butler will make use of a seemingly meaningless family ritual to steal the ancient crown of England; or that the supposed victim of a murder, a former detective himself, will in reality turn out to be the killer. It would not occur to respectable men like Watson or Lestrade that a talented, educated man could earn more by begging than by working hard at a middle-class occupation, still less that having done so he would take a country house like any successful professional man ("The Man with the Twisted Lip"). All of these discoveries require a mind free from the assumptions of comfortable, law-abiding people. In extreme cases, society can be protected only by someone who does not share its orthodoxies, who sees through the disciplines of respectability, who despite his patriotism has little reverence for popular superstitions, who stands outside the normal system of rewards and punishments, who cares nothing for status and depends only on himself—someone, in short, who has more in common with many of the criminals he discovers than with many of his clients. The paradox of Holmes's eccentricity and isolation is one of the most important things that the stories seem to assert: in order to protect the social order effectively, one must separate oneself from it. The only person we ever see defeating Holmes hands down, Irene Adler in "A Scandal in Bohemia," is also a noncriminal who lives outside the system of conventional values and behavior; she is the only woman, besides the queen, whom Holmes unreservedly admires.

A figure who is at once so able and so detached could easily seem threatening to his readers instead of comforting. Holmes is rarely or never threatening, however, because his potentially corrosive intellect never questions the basic assumptions of his society. Crime and disorder result from a failure of individual responsibility, not of institutions. Generally speaking, Holmes finds aristocrats and industrialists unappealing, but he never says a word against either aristocracy or industrialism. Unattractive noblemen, even if they seem to form a remarkably large proportion of their caste, are not to be generalized into a condemnation of the nobility as an institution; they are merely individuals. The stories are consistently hostile to war, but the thought that England's preparations and policies (the subject of several stories) might contribute to the danger of war is never voiced. This is not to say that either Holmes or his author avoids contradicting all the prejudices of the time. Sometimes opinions are approvingly expressed that much of Doyle's original audience might have found excessively tolerant. Holmes is outspokenly pro-American, for example, and in "The Yellow Face," one of the many stories that have American backgrounds, a case of interracial marriage during Reconstruction is treated as a perfectly acceptable match. In matters of the first importance to his English audience, however, Doyle on the whole kept his character from stating unorthodox views. The interracial marriage is after all set in a remote time and place, not in England.

Holmes's social philosophy, if one may so describe such a random set of attitudes, is that while the existing order of things may be unattractive in many ways, his duty and vocation is nevertheless to protect it. One has the sense that both character and author feel any general remedy would be far worse than the disease. The total effect is somewhat similar to that in such Victorian novels of reform as *Hard Times,* where a vivid, detailed description of social and economic evils is followed by a vague, pious, and unconvincing conclusion. While Doyle's purpose, unlike Dickens's, was not to encourage social change—quite the contrary—Doyle dealt with the potentially threatening implications of his stories in ways that are reminiscent of other Victorian writers who found themselves frightened by the undertones of their own realism. As Holmes's critical observations apply only to individuals, so his vocation, the solution of individual crimes, merely restores the social balance that each crime had upset. It never brings that balance into question, for the causes of disorder, where they involve more than individual motives, are not his concern.

AND YET, despite the attitudes that are so often expressed in them, the Sherlock Holmes stories are not as conservative as all that. The detective, to be sure, is by definition an upholder of the social order. But what kind of social order is presupposed by his very existence as a free-lance "highest court of appeal"— a court to whom his clients frequently appeal against the mistaken judgments of officialdom? How conservative, at bottom, is a series of books whose protagonist so often flouts both the police and the law in his determination to see that justice—the defining of which he takes to be his own individual prerogative—is finally done?

For after all, justice, not the defense of the existing order, is Holmes's ostensible aim in nearly all the stories. An exception might be made for the stories about espionage, although even here his purpose usually is not just to protect the safety of the nation but also to defend individuals who have been wrongly suspected or disgraced. More often than not, justice means not only robbing the police of their prey but showing them up as dunces. Yet doing so seems not to imperil either social stability or Holmes's own freedom of action. We have already seen that neither Holmes nor his creator shows any wish to change the workings of society in significant ways. That conservatism is a paradoxical tribute to a relatively free society, in which Holmes is free to function without interference from any official entity. No matter how many times he rescues innocent men from the police or allows guilty ones to go free, his own very wide freedom of action is never threatened. (Compare him with Nero Wolfe, whose comparable needling of the New York police leads to frequent threats that his license will be suspended, and more than once even to his arrest.) The society in which Holmes functions sets a high value on justice to individuals and has an astonishing tolerance for independent behavior. It rarely, in the stories, feels itself threatened by Holmes's treatment of the police, nor does it show any signs of ambivalence when forced to choose between upholding the prestige of Scotland Yard and doing justice to an obscure individual suspected of a crime. There are no bumperstickers, mental or otherwise, advising the people of London to support their local police. On the contrary, it is an unquestioned axiom in the stories that individuals are the locus of value, and that it *cannot* be in the interests of society for an innocent suspect, of whatever class, status, or personal character, to be punished. No matter how often Holmes shows up the police, they still call on him for help. "We're not jealous of you at Scotland Yard," Lestrade announces after Holmes has solved "The Six Napoleons." "No, sir, we are very proud of you, and if you come down tomorrow, there's not a man, from the oldest inspector to the youngest constable, who wouldn't be glad to shake you by the hand" (II, 595). Institutions are fallible; demonstrating their fallibility does not undermine them.

There is no conflict in the stories between upholding the social order and defending the rights of individuals against the power of the state, because the social order is itself a liberal one in the strict sense: the rights and liberties of individuals are among its central values. If it were not liberal, Holmes could function neither as a detective nor as a popular literary figure. What George Watson calls "the English ideology"—the belief in liberty, expressed through parliamentary institutions, as the highest political goal— is central to the stories and their popularity, whatever qualifications one might wish to make about its actual effects in English society during the age of Holmes.[7] To describe the stories as embodying "bourgeois ideology," as Stephen Knight does, is overly simple if one equates that ideology with retribution and the defense of property.[8] The contrast with British and American detective fiction after the First World War is striking.

Many kinds of justice and injustice are at issue in the stories. Not all injustices are susceptible of legal remedies. The first story of the whole series, *A Study in Scarlet*, is filled with ambiguities about crime, punishment, and the law. Its protagonist—for I doubt that either Holmes or Watson, who are present in only about two-thirds of the story, can be so described—is the murderer himself, Jefferson Hope, a romantic hero of the American frontier whose fiancée and intended father-in-law have been persecuted to their deaths by Mormons twenty years before the story proper begins. After his own escape from Utah, Hope devotes the rest of his life to avenging them, and it is the consummation of his revenge that Holmes is called in to investigate. Throughout the novel, Hope's two victims are presented as cowardly villains. Hope himself, on the contrary, is shown as courageous and resourceful both in committing his crimes and in outwitting pursuit. (His capture occurs only through an inconsistency in the plot, when he is inexplicably lured to an address that he had previously recognized as a trap.) Once he tells his own story, his implacable resistance to religious tyranny makes him the evident hero of the novel. "So thrilling had the man's narrative been," Watson declares, "and his manner was so impressive that we had sat silent and absorbed" (I, 82). Because legally constituted authority was powerless either to prevent or to avenge Hope's injuries, we are clearly intended to see his crimes as justified. As they will later be on Dartmoor, civilization and its institutions are weak forces; where their sway is lessened, or has never penetrated in the first place, superstition rules. Even London itself in this first story is a rough, chaotic place where authority is either ridiculous (the police, the press) or odious (the slumlords of south London).

In London, however, what to do with the captured Hope is a real dilemma. Doyle solves it by having him die of an aortic aneurism before he can make his appearance in court: "he was found in the morning stretched upon the floor of the cell, with a placid smile upon his face, as though he had been able in his dying moments to look back upon a useful life, and on work well done" (I, 83). Having him die in this fashion may evade the question of justice, but if one grants the initial premises of the story it becomes hard to see what else Doyle could have done. Vigilantism is intolerable in England; on the other hand, without it the crimes of twenty years ago would never have been redressed. The plot is a tale of three manhunts in which only the fittest survive and the law plays no part. *A Study in Scarlet* embodies two themes that will recur again and again in subsequent stories: the intrusion of primitivism and disorder (in this case, a medieval style of bigotry practiced in the wilderness) into the heart of civilization, and the long shadow cast upon the present by seemingly forgotten crimes committed far in the past. Contrived as it is, Jefferson Hope's natural death represents an appropriate form of justice and closure. The forces of law have been helpless bystanders throughout his career; his death enables them (and us) at least to be sympathetic bystanders at the end. A final injustice awaits us on the last page, however: Lestrade and Gregson of Scotland Yard receive credit for Hope's capture, and Holmes is described in press accounts merely as "an amateur." Newspapers, no matter how free or enterprising, are not among the forces of reason and justice that Doyle holds up to our respect.

Although Jefferson Hope manages to elude the hangman, he does not escape capture, and the device of having a sympathetic murderer die naturally before he can be tried is not one that Doyle uses again. Instead, the usual pattern in such cases is for Holmes to let the criminal go free. His habit of doing so certainly mitigates his commitment to the institutions of his society. "After all, Watson," he says after releasing a (working-class) jewel-thief in "The Blue Carbuncle," "I am not retained by the police to supply their deficiencies. . . . I suppose that I am committing a felony, but it is just possible that I am saving a soul. This fellow will not go wrong again; he is too terribly frightened. Send him to jail now, and you make him a jail-bird for life" (I, 257). In this instance, Holmes takes an enlightened view of crime, punishment, and his own duties despite the fact that the criminal in question is far from admirable. The more common pattern, however, is for him to withhold his evidence on behalf of killers in the mold of Jefferson Hope. Never again in his entire career does he turn an attractive murderer over to the police.

Doyle need not have created attractive murderers in the first place; his doing so dramatizes both the limitations of the law and the independence of his detective. In "The Abbey Grange" Holmes goes to Scotland Yard with the intention of identifying a young captain in the merchant marine who has battered in the skull of a rich, titled landowner; but he changes his mind and returns to Baker Street. "Once that warrant was made out," he explains, "nothing on earth would save him. Once or twice in my career I feel that I have done more real harm by my discovery of the criminal than ever he had done by his crime. I have learned caution now, and I had rather play tricks with the law of England than with my own conscience" (II, 646). The murderer had, it transpires, acted to protect the woman he loved from the brutality of her aristocratic husband. Holmes defends his decision a second time by contrasting his own position with that of the policeman in charge of the case: "I have the right to private judgment, but he has none. He must disclose all, or he is a traitor to his service." The implication is clear that Holmes is *not* a traitor to the cause he serves if, with some frequency, he makes his own judgment prevail over that of the authorities. Upholding the social order is not the same thing as making human sacrifices to it, still less abandoning one's own private judgment. In this story, uniquely, Holmes and Watson even go through the motions of a mock trial, in which Holmes represents the judge and Watson "a British jury, and I never met a man who was more eminently fitted to represent one" (I, 650). Responsible opinion, represented by the upright narrator, finds the killer not guilty, a judgment which Holmes sanctifies with the proverb "*Vox populi, vox Dei.*"

Respect of a sort has been paid to the forms, but in the frequent cases where they prove inadequate, justice takes priority. The same situation is repeated in "The Crooked Man," where another wife-beater meets his end at the hands of a man he had wronged decades earlier. In "The Devil's Foot," the law is doubly limited, for the killer has acted to avenge an earlier murder, undetectable by the police, of a woman whom he wished to marry but could not because of the "deplorable" divorce laws of England. In "Charles Augustus Milverton," Holmes actually witnesses the murder of a blackmailer without either preventing or reporting it. (Throughout the canon, blackmail seems to be the one unforgivable crime.) His response when Lestrade asks him to help investigate perhaps sums up one important reason that his creator made him a private rather than an official detective: "I think there are certain crimes which the law cannot touch, and which therefore, to some extent, justify private revenge. . . . My sympathies are with the criminals rather than with the victim, and I will not handle this case" (II, 582). Despite what this attitude might suggest, there is not a single case in which Holmes himself takes justice into his own hands to punish a criminal whom constituted authority cannot touch. He flouts the law only in the interests of mercy. Only in "The Speckled Band" is he even inadvertently responsible for the extralegal death of a criminal, unless we count his shooting the Hound of the Baskervilles.

Although the nature of judicial punishments is never raised as an issue in the stories, it may not be irrelevant that during Holmes's career the death penalty was the normal (although far from invariable) punishment for murder and was never, except for a few cases of treason during the First World War, invoked for any other crime. The widespread belief today that Victorian public opinion approved of execution for a wide range of offenses has no basis, for although in 1795 there had been as many as two hundred crimes which were in theory punishable by hanging, by 1837 there was in practice only one. This rapid reform came about both for humanitarian reasons and because it came to be widely recognized that the death penalty was not an effective deterrent to crime. Whatever the laws might say, in practice only a small proportion of offenders had been executed even under the older system. "Moreover," as a recent book on English crime during the eighteenth and nineteenth centuries points out,

> there is considerable evidence that the harshness of the code of laws resulted in fewer offenders being prosecuted than would otherwise have been the case. . . . Everybody in the long chain from detection of crime to final sentence, including the magistrates and judges themselves, was anxious to take every opportunity to avoid the possibility of causing one of their fellow-creatures to be executed for a mere offence against property. The victim of the crime would refrain from prosecuting. Witnesses would refuse to give evidence.
>
> Magistrates would sometimes refuse to commit people for trial despite clear-cut evidence. Juries would often bring in a perverse verdict against the facts. And the judges were ready to take advantage of every legal loophole to save the accused.[9]

Holmes's laxness in enforcing the law, particularly against people who had committed murder under mitigating circumstances, was therefore backed by a long tradition in real life. Restricting the death penalty to murder did not end the objections; strong opposition to capital punishment for any crime was voiced throughout the Victorian period, although it achieved only the limited success of abolishing public hangings in 1867.

Throughout the reign, as today, the normal punishment for serious crimes was imprisonment. We have already seen Sherlock Holmes's theory that imprisonment could turn an amateur jewel-thief into a hardened professional. The belief that most crimes were committed by members of a criminal class, and that prisons were that class's universities, coexisted uneasily (as it does today) with the desire to reform rather than merely punish. If there really was such a thing as a criminal class or subculture—and modern research suggests that Victorian opinion was not altogether mistaken in believing that there was—then prison was hardly the most effective place to combat it.[10] In fact, the belief that such a class was at the root of most crime could logically be an argument for execution and for another form of punishment that has become extinct in the Western world, transportation.

So far as Sherlock Holmes is concerned, however, the criminal-class theory might never have existed. The vast majority of the crimes he investigates are committed by middle-class people who could by no stretch of the imagination be described as professional criminals, and while he occasionally suggests that a Moriarty or a Rodger Baskerville has a "criminal streak . . . in his blood" (I, 471), he describes crime more often as random and undirected than as a predictable pattern of occurrences. Far from being a conspiracy to undermine the social order, criminal behavior is usually petty and isolated. Most of the people who engage in it do so partly because of circumstances over which they have little control. Such conventional scapegoats as gipsies are sometimes suspected of serious crimes (for example, in "Silver Blaze" and "The Priory School"), but they always turn out to be innocent. The secret political societies that pop up so often in the stories are colorful, but not even the police ever regard them as a serious threat to English society; mostly they work ineffectually to overthrow various Continental despotisms. The Mafia appears once ("The Six Napoleons") as an exotic curiosity. Moriarty as a Napoleon of crime is not merely rare but unique in the stories, and after his death Holmes laments the fact that "London has become a singularly uninteresting city" (II, 496). It was widely, and apparently correctly, believed in the late nineteenth century that crime was a less serious problem than it had been a hundred years earlier.[11] Sherlock Holmes frequently complains that "audacity and romance seem to have passed forever from the criminal world" (II, 870), and that "the London criminal is certainly a dull fellow" (II, 913). Under these circumstances, protecting the social order does not require very draconian measures, at least in the pursuit of crime. The detective and society alike can afford to be magnanimous much of the time.

Earlier criminals were not so fortunate, and we are meant to see English society in the stories as more enlightened and humane than it had been even as recently as the 1850s. Not only public hanging, but transportation—the removal of convicts to forced labor in the Australian colonies—was part of the repertoire of punishments three decades before *A Study in Scarlet*.[12] James Trevor, in "The Gloria Scott," supposedly Holmes's very first case, was transported for committing an embezzlement which, like so many crimes in the stories, was a consequence more of weakness and ill luck than of malicious intentions. "The case might have been dealt leniently with," he aptly explains, "but the laws were more harshly administered thirty years ago than now, and on my twenty-third birthday I found myself chained as a felon with thirty-seven other convicts in the 'tween-decks of the bark *Gloria Scott*, bound for Australia" (I, 381).

As is so often the case in the stories, injustice leads to consequences far worse than the original crime, and secrets in the remote past bring disaster in the present. Subjected to inhuman conditions, the prisoners of the *Gloria Scott* mutiny, massacre the crew, and (with a few exceptions) accidentally blow themselves up. The survivors make their way to Australia, predictably strike it rich in the gold fields, and return to England under assumed names. But secrets will out, and many years later—while Holmes is supposed to be an undergraduate—a villainous seaman named Hudson, whom the surviving mutineers had saved, returns to blackmail Trevor. Thus over a period of twenty-five years or so, roles are reversed: the embezzler, mutineer, and escaped convict becomes a sympathetic figure (not to mention a wealthy and respected one), while an innocent young sailor proves to be thoroughly odious. We are even encouraged (by Holmes) to believe at the end of the story that Hudson has blessedly been murdered by another of the surviving mutineers. Law and order become wholly unattractive when they produce injustice; they even, Doyle seems to suggest, become dangerous to the very stability they represent.

Although "The Gloria Scott" dates from 1893 and is therefore an early story, Doyle had already begun to repeat himself, for the same plot had appeared with minor variations in "The Boscombe Valley Mystery" (1891). Evidently it represented a pattern that Doyle found compelling. Once again we have a wealthy, aging man, this time named McCarthy, who made his money long ago in the Australian gold fields and returned to England to live out his life as a country squire. It is not clear whether McCarthy had originally been transported, but his way of life in Australia was that of a criminal: having failed to strike it rich as a miner, he took up highway robbery and murder. Again the blackmailer is a formerly law-abiding man whom he had spared, this time in the robbery of a "gold convoy." As in "The Gloria Scott," our sympathy for the former criminal is firmly established before we ever learn the history of his relations with the blackmailer, Turner. In this case, the crime that Holmes has been called in to investigate is the brutal murder of Turner ("The head had been beaten in by repeated blows of some heavy and blunt weapon"), which proves in the end to have been committed by McCarthy. As in other cases that involve blackmail or reach far into the past, Holmes's notion of justice owes little to the law and less to the Old Testament. "God help us!" he exclaims after letting the murderer go free. "Why does fate play such tricks with poor, helpless worms? I never hear of such a case as this that I do not think of Baxter's words, and say, 'There, but for the grace of God, goes Sherlock Holmes'" (I, 217).

A character who behaves this way can hardly be described as a symbol of social conservatism and the sanctity of property. His concern is justice, and if by and large he takes the institutions of late-Victorian England as given, he reserves to his own judgment the complicated questions of what constitutes justice in a given set of circumstances and how far it involves bringing people who have committed crimes to the notice of those institutions. Both his detection and his magnanimity derive in part from egotism and from pleasure in the exercise of his powers; they are also, as we see in this last quotation, an expression of humaneness and humility that accords well with the period's prevailing notions.

VICTORIAN WRITERS from Disraeli to Dickens, from Tennyson to Arnold to Huxley, were almost obsessively aware of chaos lurking below the surface of civilized life, waiting for the opportunity to reassert itself. Not only the order of society but civilization it-self was a precarious creation, maintained with immense effort against continuous threats. The theory of evolution gave to this pervasive fear a form that was at once scientific and iconographic, for the anarchic and bestial appetites that were so inimical to order could now be seen as survivals of primitive life, of the time when man was half an ape. Reason, morality, law, love, art—all the qualities that made civilization possible were late develop-ments in the evolution of the species, and their hold on human-kind was as yet so tenuous that the slightest emergency might reestablish the control of older, darker forces. "Move upward, working out the beast, / And let the ape and tiger die," Tennyson had counseled in *In Memoriam*. Much Victorian opinion cried "Amen!" to the sentiment; only an optimistic few were at all confident that the ape and tiger had yet died out of human nature. "The highest type of man may revert to the animal if he leaves the straight road of destiny," as Sherlock Holmes puts it in "The Creeping Man" (II, 1082).

Among the literary expressions of this set of attitudes, *The Hound of the Baskervilles* (1902) is one of the masterpieces. It is the most highly symbolic of all the Sherlock Holmes stories and the most carefully constructed of the novels. The phosphorescent hound itself, hurtling inexorably across the foggy wastes of Dartmoor after its victim, is the most powerful figure of horror in all the literature of crime, an apparition worthy to threaten not just the existing order of society but the order of the rational mind itself. It is fitting that the threat should manifest itself not in Holmes's own London, the capital of the civilized world, but in a remote rural area among the ruined dwellings of prehistoric man.

Holmes's predilection for London and anti-romantic mistrust of the countryside are made clear from the start of his career and never change. London is the locus of all those aspects of civilization and intellectual progess that he values most highly. Rural England, on the other hand, has never altogether evolved out of barbarism. The ape and tiger retain a stronger hold there; law and reason are correspondingly frailer. Holmes makes his feelings clear in the early story "The Copper Beeches": "It is my belief, Watson, founded upon my experience, that the lowest and vilest alleys in London do not present a more dreadful record of sin than does the smiling and beautiful countryside" (I, 323). He might have added that in the country, as this story and others illustrate, the squire is a nearly absolute power and may be an absolute tyrant; neither law nor public opinion is strong enough to bridle him, and geographic isolation sometimes permits him to get away with murder. In *The Hound of the Baskervilles* we are never allowed to forget the contrasts between London and Dartmoor, and it is only by submitting to live for a time in a pre-historic stone hut on the moor that Holmes's London mind can defeat and partially exorcise the primitive forces arrayed against his client.

The early chapters of the book are heavy with references to nightmare, madness, the diabolical, and reversions to the primitive. Dr. Mortimer, who brings the case to Holmes's attention, is an archeologist and a specialist in atavistic diseases. His two published papers are significantly entitled "Some Freaks of Atavism" and "Do We Progress?" A man of scientific habits, and London-trained, he finds himself wholly at a loss to understand the story he tells Holmes of the mysterious death of Sir Charles Baskerville. A "spectral hound," a "hound of hell" in the England of 1889?[13] Yet he has seen the footprints in the yew alley beside the body of his friend. Having read Holmes the centuries-old legend of the nemesis hound, he does not know whether the tools of science will have any power to explain the horror on the moor. At the same time, he has won Holmes's respect by calculating the length of time Sir Charles had waited at the moor gate from the number of times ash had dropped from his cigar. "It is evidently a case of extraordinary interest," Holmes declares, "and one which presented immense opportunities to the scientific expert." Dr. Mortimer is more doubtful.

> "There is a realm in which the most acute and most experienced of detectives is helpless."
> "You mean that the thing is supernatural?"
> "I did not positively say so."
> "No, but you evidently think it."

Holmes's reaction is comfortingly skeptical:

> "I have hitherto confined my investigations to this world," said he. "In a modest way I have combated evil, but to take on the Father of Evil himself would, perhaps, be too ambitious a task. Yet you must admit that the footmark is material." (II, 680−81)

Soon Holmes prepares himself for the investigation of the case and the protection of the new baronet, Sir Henry Baskerville, who has just come back from the wide, empty spaces of western Canada to take up residence at Baskerville Hall. Needless to say, Sir Henry has no conception of what awaits him in the corrupt old world of his ancestors. A conversation with Watson foreshadows what is to come but hardly prepares us adequately for it. Watson comments:

"It must be a wild place."
"Yes, the setting is a worthy one. If the devil did desire to have a hand in the affairs of men—"
"Then you are yourself inclining to the supernatural explanation."
"The devil's agents may be of flesh and blood, may they not? . . . Of course, if Dr. Mortimer's surmise should be correct, and we are dealing with forces outside the ordinary laws of Nature, there is an end of our investigation. But we are bound to exhaust all other hypotheses before falling back upon this one. . . ." (II, 684)

The sense of foreboding, of menacing forces that transcend the ordinary powers of crime, increases markedly once the focus of the story shifts to Dartmoor. Holmes has already remarked, "I am not sure that of all the five hundred cases of capital importance which I have handled there is one which cuts so deep" (II, 693). When Watson approaches Baskerville Hall, we begin to wonder whether Holmes may this time be out of his depth. The very landscape conspires against rationality. "Over the green squares of the fields and the low curve of a wood," the normally unimaginative Watson describes gothically, "there rose in the distance a gray, melancholy hill, with a strange jagged summit, dim and vague in the distance, like some fantastic landscape in a dream." It is autumn. "The rattle of our wheels died away as we drove through drifts of rotting vegetation . . ." (II, 700–701). The nightmare landscape is not altogether uninhabited. Amid the bleakness stand the houses of Sir Henry's few neighbors and, farther away, the great prison of Princetown. There are soldiers on the road because a prisoner has escaped—a savage murderer, perhaps insane, with "beetling forehead . . . sunken animal eyes," "half animal and half demon" (II, 745, 748). A throwback to the primitive who might have stepped from one of Dr. Mortimer's papers, he is an appropriate inhabitant of this landscape, and it is fitting as well as chilling that after living for a time on the moor, he breaks his neck while trying to escape from the Hound.

At the center of this haunted wasteland, reducing even the Princetown prison to insignificance, is the great Grimpen Mire. "A false step yonder means death to man or beast," declares Stapleton, the naturalist, and Watson witnesses at a distance the death of a pony that has been caught in its grip. The pathways to the islands at the center of the bog are mysterious and dangerous; Stapleton warns Watson against trying to find his way there, adding, "That is where the rare plants and the butterflies are, if you have the wit to reach them" (II, 707–8). As we learn eventually, the Hound of the Baskervilles is there too, awaiting the night when his master will have need of him. Meanwhile, the moor has become a place of horror to the local peasants, haunted by the sound of his baying, and even steadier observers find that the mire has taken hold of their minds. "Life has become like that great Grimpen Mire," Watson says soon after his arrival, "with little green patches everywhere into which one may sink and with no guide to point the track" (II, 711).

By the end of the story, the rational mind is back on its throne, and the spectral hound is only a dead dog. But the outcome does not erase the impression of horror and unreason that has been so powerfully built up. Nor is it easily reached. Before it comes, Holmes must undergo an initiation by living on the moor, actually sleeping on the stone bed of vanished prehistoric inhabitants, and Sir Henry must confront the Hound alone, an experience that costs him a nervous breakdown. The forces of order and civilization are pitifully weak. The soldiers never come close to capturing the convict; indeed, they never appear again in the story. The police are never in evidence until Holmes summons them at the end. The local embodiment of the law is ridiculous: an eccentric landowner who indulges in petty lawsuits as a sport. No clergyman ever calls at Baskerville Hall. Dr. Mortimer is amiable but perennially baffled. Sir Henry, the local squire and symbol of order, is surrounded by malevolence. Even servants betray him, both in London and at Baskerville Hall. And Stapleton, the man of science, proves to be the trainer of the Hound, the murderer of Sir Charles, the disguised next heir to the baronetcy, and a throwback to the most evil of all the Baskervilles.

The Hound of the Baskervilles is in fact a story of throwbacks from beginning to end. Civilization is not merely fragile; its representatives are paralyzed. Stapleton nearly wins, for he is masterful, imaginative, wholly unscrupulous, and more purposeful than any other character in the story except Holmes. Since Holmes is absent from nearly half the story—living out on the moor when Watson believes him to be in London—Watson and the reader alike have a frustrating sense of being at war with forces that are menacing, unerringly directed, and impossible to identify. Only when Holmes reappears, discovered by Watson in his stone hut on the moor, does the situation begin to clarify. When Watson notes that Holmes's chin was "as smooth and his linen as perfect as if he were in Baker Street" (II, 740), we know that civilization will win, though thanks only to a single champion.

Even at that, the moor almost defeats Holmes. When he orders Sir Henry to walk home at night as bait for the Hound and its master, a dense fog drifts across the path. Holmes, Watson, and Lestrade are forced to retreat to higher ground, and when they finally see the Hound, it is nearly upon its victim. Once again, everyone is paralyzed except the detective himself. Watson describes the spectacle:

> A hound it was, an enormous coal-black hound, but not such a
> hound as mortal eyes have ever seen. Fire burst from its open

mouth, its eyes glowed with a smouldering glare, its muzzle and hackles and dewlap were outlined in flickering flame. Never in the delirious dream of a disordered brain could anything more savage, more appalling, more hellish be conceived than that dark form and savage face which broke upon us out of the wall of fog. (II, 757)

Holmes manages, just barely, to shoot the Hound and save his client's life. Stapleton escapes from Holmes and the law but apparently falls victim to the mire. Primitive nature, not the forces of order, reclaims him in the end.

Holmes ultimately defeats Stapleton through what he calls "the scientific use of the imagination" (II, 687), and it is an impressive victory. Stapleton is the most powerful antagonist Holmes ever faces—"never yet have we helped to hunt down a more dangerous man than he who is lying yonder" (II, 760), he tells Watson near the end. Like Moriarty, who in the somewhat murky chronology of the stories is supposed not to have appeared on the scene yet, Stapleton is dangerous partly because he too represents the scientific intellect married to a Holmesian degree of determination. (He is, however, a much more realized and less abstract character than Moriarty.) He has become a dedicated student of the moor, and Holmes must do the same in order to defeat him. All the other characters appear puny and powerless in the setting of Dartmoor. One has the feeling that Holmes and Stapleton are equals who understand each other all along. On one occasion, Stapleton even impersonates Holmes. As Stapleton, his plans, and his hound are repeatedly described as diabolical, so Holmes is once half-consciously referred to by Watson as "our guardian angel" (II, 739). Their combat is inevitable and without quarter. Each is immensely resourceful but lonely, aided only by smaller figures who do not understand what they are doing. Each, in fact, deceives his closest associate.

The victory is won, the demons are exorcised; Holmes's solution to the mystery vindicates science and civilization. "We've laid the family ghost once and forever," he announces at the moment of triumph (II, 757). But it is only a partial triumph, for the bleakness of Dartmoor and the mire remains as impenetrable and unconquerable as any Wessex landscape in the novels of Thomas Hardy. Stapleton is apparently dead, but his legacy of malice survives him, for we have learned that he used to run a school. As he told it himself soon after meeting Watson, "The privilege of living with youth, of helping to mould those young minds, and of impressing them with one's own character and ideals was very dear to me" (II, 710). Seldom is Conan Doyle quite so ironic as this, but then seldom in the Holmes stories are the issues as large as they are here. Sir Henry, instead of entering into the enjoyment of his inheritance, has had to leave the country for a year's convalescent travel with Dr. Mortimer. Holmes, needless to say, is back in London, center of the world he represents. As the story ends, he is about to celebrate his commitment to civilization in an entirely appropriate and symbolic fashion—by taking Watson to the opera.

AFTER *The Hound of the Baskervilles,* Conan Doyle published only one more Sherlock Holmes novel—*The Valley of Fear* (1914), a second-rate thriller in which Holmes appears only at the beginning and end—and three collections of short stories. In two late stories, "The Devil's Foot" and "The Sussex Vampire," he tried to recapture the resonance and conviction of *The Hound of the Baskervilles,* but both stories are relative failures. The short-story form did not permit sufficient development to make the exorcism of the irrational fully persuasive. Furthermore, Doyle had by now grown tired of Holmes and Watson. Few of the stories in *His Last Bow* (1917) and almost none in *The Case Book of Sherlock Holmes* (1927), the last two collections, have anything like the depth or richness of even the less ambitious stories in the earlier volumes.

Perhaps Doyle's waning interest is sufficient to explain the decline, but there is another reason with effects that reached beyond Doyle. I have already pointed out that the seriousness and impact of the Holmes canon depended on the belief, shared by author and readers, that crime represented a potentially mortal threat to civilization and that the isolated but loyal detective was the only figure equipped to meet it. Early in the twentieth century, both halves of this belief became less plausible. The police (in England, at least) came to be more highly respected than before, and crime came to seem less pervasive and threatening.[14] By the time of the late stories, the police have improved to the point that in "The Red Circle" and "Wisteria Lodge," they figure things out more thoroughly than the now superfluous Holmes. But I offer the speculation that the First World War was the crucial event that made the detective story a less serious form of entertainment than it had been at Holmes's peak. After 1918, it was no longer easy for a serious writer to believe that domestic crime was among the most important threats to the stability of civilization. War, revolution, and foreign enemies had permanently replaced it. Who could regard a solitary murderer, or even a Napoleon of crime, with the same gravity in an age of world wars and political upheavals?[15]

From the 1870s until 1914, there had been a flourishing genre of popular fiction that dealt with the probable course of a future great war between Britain and Germany, or sometimes between Britain and France. Conan Doyle even contributed to this kind of fiction with a story called "Danger," which warned that German submarine warfare could imperil British supply routes in the event of a European war. Instead of preparing their readers for the realities of modern world war, however, most of the books and stories of this kind had the opposite effect, for they assumed that the wars of the future would be much like the brief wars of the mid-nineteenth century. I. F. Clarke, who has studied this genre exhaustively, declares:

It became standard practice for writers in the major European countries to describe the shape of the war-to-come in order to demonstrate the need for bigger armies or better warships. . . . Almost all of them took it for granted that the next war would be fought more or less after the style of the last, and that war would continue to be conducted in a relatively restrained and humane manner. . . . The slaughter of the trenches, the use of poison gas, the immense damage caused by submarines, the very scale of a world-wide industrialized war were mercifully hidden from the admirals, generals, politicians, and popular novelists who joined in the great enterprise of predicting what was going to happen.[16]

When the *real* war came, its horror took everyone by surprise. Among the many things it swept away was the set of beliefs about civilization, and the threats to civilization, that underlay the creation of a hero like Sherlock Holmes.

One has the sense, in reading the late Holmes stories, of watching a play near the end of its run that has transferred to a smaller theatre. The wooden repetition of earlier plots in late stories like "The Mazarin Stone" and "Shoscombe Old Place" leads one to think that Doyle had not only tired of his characters but no longer felt that crime was very important. As Doyle became more and more devoted to spiritualism during and after the war, so Holmes in the late stories grows increasingly frustrated, as if conscious of the small scope in which his powers are effectual. "The ways of fate are indeed hard to understand," he exclaims in "The Veiled Lodger." "If there is not some compensation hereafter, then the world is a cruel jest" (II, 1101). In "The Retired Colourman," the final story in the last collection, he is even more wistful: "But is not all life pathetic and futile? . . . We reach. We grasp. And what is left in our hands at the end? A shadow. Or worse than a shadow—misery" (II, 1113). The Holmes who makes these statements is still a genius who solves crimes that baffle the police, but he has come a long way from the eager crusader who had just discovered a test for bloodstains.

In the preface to the last collection, where he bade farewell to Holmes and Watson, Doyle conjured up "some fantastic limbo for the children of imagination" and expressed the hope that "perhaps in some humble corner of such a Valhalla, Sherlock and his Watson may for a time find a place, while some more astute sleuth with some even less astute comrade may fill the stage which they have vacated" (II, 983). The successors duly made their entrances—indeed, Hercule Poirot was already before the footlights—but the stage proved to be a smaller one than before, with sets that were more obviously artificial. Agatha Christie, Margery Allingham, Dorothy Sayers, Cyril Hare, and their contemporaries all wrote superlatively well at times, but often it is hard not to feel that they regarded murder as a joke and an opportunity for clever twists of plot. Perhaps it had become too rare in real English life to be treated any other way. There are exceptions in the work of all these writers, but rarely do they take crime, its social context, or its implications as seriously as Doyle did in the stories that made Sherlock Holmes one of the most famous characters in the world's literature.[17] Their detectives remain guardians of conservative values in whom irony, eccentricity for its own sake, and upper-class affectations replace the earnestness of the Holmes stories. This problem of seriousness is sometimes dealt with by involving them in counterespionage, but as several of the Holmes stories had already demonstrated, the solitary detective's talents were incongruent with the scale of international relations. Much of the detective fiction written since 1945 is superior in character development to all that went before, but it lacks the social and moral resonance of Doyle at his best. A character like Sherlock Holmes could grow to full stature only in a time when crime could plausibly be seen as the greatest threat to order and its detection the greatest of services, when the police were widely believed to be ineffectual, when science was viewed by its enthusiasts as a new force crusading for progress against ignorance and unreason—above all, when the prospect of a devastating war could seem less menacing than an unsolved robbery or murder.

5. J. R. R. Tolkien:
The Monsters and the Critics

I T IS NOW more than thirty years since J. R. R. Tolkien, an Oxford philologist previously known to the scholarly world for a penetrating essay on *Beowulf* and to the public as the author of a children's book called *The Hobbit*, published a three-volume work of fiction entitled *The Lord of the Rings*, complete with maps and appendices detailing the geography, history, and languages of an imaginary world called Middle-earth. To say that the literary world of the 1950s did not know what to make of Tolkien's opus would be putting it mildly. The knowing, cynical, anti-traditional decade of *Lucky Jim* (published in the same year as Tolkien's first two volumes, *The Fellowship of the Ring* and *The Two Towers*) hardly seemed the time for heroic fable, or whatever *Lord of the Rings* might be. When the final volume, *The Return of the King*, appeared after several delays in 1955, critical response to the completed work was immediately polarized. For one group of critics, including C. S. Lewis, W. H. Auden, and Louis Halle, Tolkien had produced a masterpiece of twentieth-century literature, a work that rivalled (and had much in common with) *Le Morte d'Arthur* and *The Faerie Queen*. To another group, represented by Edwin Muir and Edmund Wilson, *Lord of the Rings* was an overgrown, ineptly constructed children's book filled with undeveloped characters, organized around a series of incidents that compelled no belief, motivated by reactionary social attitudes, and written in an archaic fustian reminiscent of Victorian imitations of Malory.

Pro-Tolkien critics tended to express themselves in extremes. "The book is too original and too opulent for any final judgment on a first reading," C. S. Lewis declared. "But we know at once that it has done things to us. We are not quite the same men."[1] W. H. Auden added: "If there is any Quest Tale which, while primarily concerned with the subjective life of the individual person as all such stories must be, manages to do more justice to our experience of social-historical realities than *The Lord of the Rings,* I should be glad to hear of it."[2] The prosecution was no less definite. Edmund Wilson announced that except when Tolkien "is being pedantic and also boring the adult reader, there is little in *The Lord of the Rings* over the head of a seven-year-old child." He ridiculed the language and characterizations of the book and then delivered a series of criticisms that were essentially moral: "What we get here is a simple confrontation—in more or less the traditional terms of British melodrama—of the Forces of Evil with the Forces of Good, the remote and alien villain with the plucky little home-grown hero. . . ." Lewis had warned against the mistake of seeing the main characters in black-and-white terms, but Wilson was not impressed. "There are Black Riders, of whom everyone is terrified but who never seem anything but specters. There are dreadful hovering birds—think of it, horrible birds of prey! There are ogreish disgusting Orcs, who, however, rarely get to the point of committing any overt acts. There is a giant female spider—a dreadful creepy-crawly spider!—who lives in a dark cave and eats people." Summing up this particular line of criticism, Wilson concluded, "The wars are never dynamic; the ordeals give no sense of strain; the fair ladies would not stir a heartbeat; the horrors would not hurt a fly." He ends by accounting for the popularity of the book with critics in the other camp by surmising that "certain people—especially, perhaps, in Britain—have a lifelong appetite for juvenile trash."[3]

In the three decades since *Lord of the Rings* appeared, the literary and moral climates have changed almost out of recognition. Tolkien, Lewis, Auden, and Wilson have all passed from the scene. In the sixties and early seventies, Tolkien's work was the object of a cult that made the names of its characters household words and probably damaged its literary reputation, although the long-term effects of its popularity are hard to judge. A vast amount of scholarship and criticism, much of it by hobbyists, has elucidated *Lord of the Rings, The Hobbit,* and *The Silmarillion,* Tolkien's posthumous history of the Elves. The author has been the subject of an excellent biography by Humphrey Carpenter, who has also edited a lengthy volume of his letters. Yet critical opinion of *Lord of the Rings* has not changed much since the 1950s. As Carpenter characterizes it, "extreme praise from one faction, total contempt from the other" dominated critical discussion until Tolkien's death in 1973, and ever since.[4]

Not only is there no consensus on the merits of *Lord of the Rings,* there is not even agreement as to what kind of work it is. Because it was published in three volumes, like many Victorian novels, it is often wrongly referred to as a trilogy; but trilogy of what? Some critics describe it as an epic, others as a romance. It bears little resemblance to any epic or romance of the past, however, and the use of such faded terminology disguises the fact that it could only have been written in the mid-twentieth century. "Fantasy," largely through its application to the work of Tolkien and his imitators, has become little more than a vague honorific.

In fact *Lord of the Rings* is a novel, one drawn from many disparate sources but a novel nonetheless, embodying most of the technical features associated with novels since the eighteenth century—even a realistic novel for most of its length, provided that "realism" is understood as a set of conventions for the delineation of plot and character rather than as a theory about the world. It is furthermore an identifiably modernist novel, one that incorporates myth and a variety of elements from the distant literary past in a self-conscious way to achieve a wholly new creation. In conception, it bears a closer resemblance to *The Waste Land* than to any medieval Arthurian work. Although it is set in a remote period of imaginary history—I shall give below some reasons for describing it as prehistory—the alert reader is never allowed to forget the twentieth century and its dilemmas of totalitarian power, technological obliteration, and individual choice. With occasional exceptions, the source-hunting to which *Lord of the Rings* has driven baffled scholars and critics is as futile as the footnoting of T. S. Eliot's literary allusions. The meaning of the book (a complicated meaning, reducible to no simple set of assertions) has to do with twentieth-century problems and is directed at twentieth-century readers.

It is precisely the contemporary significance of *Lord of the Rings,* however subliminally apprehended, that has led to the polarization of opinion about it. Of all the attacks made on it, the most implausible is the charge of escapism. Far from encouraging us to take refuge in a world of dreamy Elves, *Lord of the Rings* is a book with moral and social designs on its readers. A comparison with *The Silmarillion,* which really is dominated by dreamy Elves, is enlightening. That book, which Tolkien worked on desultorily for half a century and never finished, was a disappointment to everyone but a few fanatics when the author's son Christopher published a version of it in 1977. What it lacks is human concerns that have any bearing on contemporary life. *Lord of the Rings* is altogether a different kind of work, and in praising or attacking it critics tend not surprisingly to focus on the moral and social positions which it seems to embody. Those who admire the book praise it for showing us powerful examples of heroism, courage, loyalty, determination, and—an explicitly twentieth-century virtue—environmental sensitivity. Those who attack it do so because they consider it authoritarian, militaristic, snobbish or worse in its apparently unquestioning acceptance of hereditary inequalities, condescending at best in its portrayal of women, shallow in its characterizations, and above all morally simplistic in its description of a war to the death between good and evil.

The last two charges are closely related. In moral allegory, it has always been one of the conventions that characterization may remain on the level of saints (for example, Gandalf) and heroes (for example, Aragorn) versus monsters (for example, Sauron and his Orcs) provided that some moral illumination occurs. But moral allegory is on the whole offensive to modern tastes, and Tolkien denies with some heat that *Lord of the Rings* has any allegorical intentions.[5] He was perfectly happy, however, to tell Naomi Mitchison in 1954 that "the story is cast in terms of a good side, and a bad side, beauty against ruthless ugliness, tyranny against kingship, moderated freedom with consent against compulsion that has long lost any object save mere power, and so on."[6] It is, of course, possible to believe, as C. S. Lewis maintained in reviewing the book, that human life involves warfare between objective goods and evils without maintaining that actual people are altogether one or the other. It is also possible, as Tolkien himself suggested in his long essay "On Fairy-Stories," to think that modern literature suffers from being anthropocentric, and that critics overemphasize characterization at the expense of other values.[7]

Nonetheless, such critics of Tolkien as Edmund Wilson, Catharine R. Stimpson, and Burton Raffel have prepared a forceful indictment.[8] Examining *Lord of the Rings* in some detail with these charges in mind should help us decide what sort of novel it is as well as how good, even though its moral content is far from the only issue involved in deciding either question. "It is frankly an impossibility," declares Robert Giddings, one of Tolkien's hostile critics, "to regard *Lord of the Rings* simply and purely as a fine piece of writing, devoid of political, economic or ideological significance."[9] This is perfectly true, so long as the last phrase is defined broadly enough. Only an extreme formalist or someone who shared the attitudes in question would deny that insofar as the indictment outlined above is accurate, the charges it summarizes are damaging ones. How true are they? What was Tolkien about, and what did he accomplish?

In a 1954 letter to the manager of a Catholic bookshop in Oxford, Tolkien declared that the purposes of *Lord of the Rings* were "largely literary (and, if you don't boggle at the term, didactic)." He went on to ask himself a general question about the kind of literary invention that he had long ago christened "subcreation":

> Are there any 'bounds to a writer's job' except those imposed by his own finiteness? No bounds, but the laws of contradiction, I should think. But, of course, humility and an awareness of peril is required. A writer may be basically 'benevolent' according to his lights (as I hope I am) and yet not be 'beneficent' owing to error and stupidity. I would claim, if I did not think it presumptuous in one so ill-instructed, to have as one object the elucidation of truth, and the encouragement of good morals in this real world, by the ancient device of exemplifying them in unfamiliar embodiments, that may tend to 'bring them home'. But, of course, I may be in error (at some or all points): my truths may not be true, or they may be distorted: and the mirror I have made may be dim and cracked. But I should need to be fully convinced that anything I have 'feigned' is actually harmful, *per se* and not merely because misunderstood, before I should recant or rewrite anything.[10]

The story that this statement describes has two dominant motifs. One is the progressive discovery, not only by the hobbits who are at the center of it but also by other characters whom they encounter, of the complicated world they live in. The other is a struggle against totalitarian evil in which a precarious victory is finally won but found to be neither permanent nor complete: some good things disappear from the world forever. The two motifs may be combined in the observation that Middle-earth is peopled with an astonishing variety of beings—some good, some bad, most mixed—and nothing in it lasts forever. Hence the length and inventiveness of the book, for each of these peoples has its own history, view of the world, and provincial concerns.

Provinciality is a major issue from the beginning. The hobbits of the Shire, that tidy section of pastoral Warwickshire set down in the northwest of Middle-earth, are a home-loving folk with many virtues, but curiosity about the outside world is not one of them. As we learn early, "they heeded less and less the world outside where dark things moved, until they came to think that peace and plenty were the rule in Middle-earth and the right of all sensible folk. . . . They were, in fact, sheltered, but they had ceased to remember it" (I, 14). As hostile critics frequently point out, the hobbits resemble children in this and other respects, most obviously their height, which is about half that of a grown man. Their childish provinciality makes them engaging characters on the whole, but it also makes them defenseless against unaccustomed dangers. To this general characterization, there are only five exceptions in the story—hobbits who, in a variety of ways, grow up. The first is Bilbo Baggins, protagonist of *The Hobbit*, who at the beginning of *Lord of the Rings* leaves the Shire forever to live with the more cosmopolitan Elves of Rivendell. The other four are Bilbo's nephew Frodo, Frodo's cousins Merry and Pippin, and his servant Sam, whose adventures form most of the plot of *Lord of the Rings*.

Their education begins when they leave the Shire, pursued by Black Riders who are the servants of Sauron, the Dark Lord of Mordor. (The first of the story's many monsters, they are nine men who long ago became Ringwraiths, or Nazgul, and are now searching for the One Ring of Power, which has, through a complicated series of events, come into Frodo's possession by way of Bilbo.) "I knew that danger lay ahead, of course," Frodo complains naively to an Elf; "but I did not expect to meet it in our own Shire." The answer opens up a larger, older world to the unsuspecting hobbits: "But it is not your own Shire. Others dwelt here before hobbits were; and others will dwell here again when hobbits are no more. The wide world is all about you: you can fence yourselves in, but you cannot for ever fence it out" (I, 93). The lesson is a painful one, both for the four hobbits who learn it by going away and for the rest who stay home, fall easy prey to a petty dictator's invasion, and have to be delivered at the end from the results of their own ignorance. The fact that hobbits often behave like children is an important element in the story's design. Humility, personal loyalty, and the openness to experience that makes education possible are also qualities found in children, and the hobbits who accompany Frodo on his journey have large measures of all three. It should be noted that their education, like all their major actions, is freely chosen; Gandalf, Aragorn, and Elrond all scrupulously avoid compelling them to do anything.

The journey of discovery consumes three volumes and is as tightly organized as any plot of comparable length in all of fiction. On the first stage of their travels, the hobbits are filled with a naive wonder that makes more than one of the people they encounter doubtful about their prospects for getting much farther. "Well, you do want looking after and no mistake: your party might be on a holiday!" comments the innkeeper at Bree (I, 181). Their first adventures are little more than a series of rescues, first by the mysterious Tom Bombadil in the Old Forest, then at Bree by a rather insecure-seeming man named Strider. By the time they reach the temporary security of Rivendell, they have developed into more experienced travellers in the wide world; but meantime Frodo has been wounded by a Nazgul because of his folly in putting on the Ring of Power, an event that foreshadows his ultimate claiming of it on Mount Doom. The enemies they meet in this part of the story—Ringwraiths, the Willow, and Barrow-wights—are all nonhuman in the ordinary sense of the word, as are the Elves and Tom Bombadil. As a result the hobbits are rapidly losing their arrogant sense that man (or hobbit) is the measure of all things. This realization is one of the moral themes that Tolkien placed at the heart of the work; it is strengthened later on when Merry and Pippin live for a while with the Ents, one of Tolkien's most effective creations.

By that time, the journey of discovery has become a less simple process. In fact it has become two processes, for Frodo and Sam are by this time trudging through the deserts of Mordor. The hobbits have become a catalyst through whose action the peoples of Middle-earth, from Elves to Ents to Riders of Rohan to wild men in the woods, discover each other's existence. This mutual overcoming of isolation is hastened by Sauron's war of universal conquest. As war spreads and the events of the story become more apocalyptic, the by now experienced hobbits are among the least surprised at each new encounter. They, of course, have the advantage of knowing about the Ring, that symbol of a tempting and altogether destructive absolute power which has precipitated the war. But they have also achieved a stature that other characters recognize on meeting them for the first time. Treebeard, who shares with Tom Bombadil the uncertain distinction of being the oldest creature in Middle-earth, is shaken out of his own provinciality when Merry and Pippin bring him news of the war (II, 75ff.). Theoden, the king of Rohan, meets the same two hobbits before the ruins of Isengard and exclaims: "The days are fated to be filled with marvels. Already I have seen many since I left my house; and now here before my eyes stand yet another of the folk of legend" (II, 163). The process of education has come full circle: the discoverers are now a discovery.

The peoples they encounter have a variety of symbolic functions in the total design. The Elves represent a certain kind of wisdom, but they live in the past and have little to offer but moral support. The victory over Sauron, in which they play small part, will mean the end of their life in Middle-earth, and they know it. While they are certainly on the side of good, the good that they embody is attenuated. They die no natural deaths and are tormented by memory. As Tolkien put it in a letter the year the first two volumes were published, "They wanted to have their cake and eat it: to live in the mortal historical Middle-earth because they had become fond of it (and perhaps because they there had the advantages of a superior caste), and so tried to stop its change and history, stop its growth, keep it as a pleasaunce, even largely a desert, where they could be 'artists'—and they were overburdened with sadness and nostalgic regret."[11] The Ents likewise have declined from the days when the forests over which they rule covered most of Middle-earth. Abandoned by the Entwives, with no way now to reproduce themselves, threatened alike by agriculture and by industry, they are a fading race, and only the immediate threat of extinction posed by Saruman stirs them up to take part in the war—nature revenging itself, so to speak. (Industrialism, represented by both Sauron and Saruman, is a major target of the whole book; Saruman has turned Isengard into a nineteenth-century company town, and when he briefly rules the Shire he cuts down as many trees as possible and builds what seem to be factories.) Like the Elves, the Ents will gradually disappear after the Third Age comes to an end. The Riders of Rohan, on the contrary, represent youth—as Faramir, a man of Gondor, tells Frodo and Sam, "They remind us of the youth of Men, as they were in the Elder Days" (II, 287). They still have a future. The same is true of Faramir's people, who represent a higher human civilization, decayed from its greatest days but energetic enough to renew itself. All of these peoples are capable of both good and evil acts, as we see in the story; only humans seem to be still capable of growth.

The fate of hobbits as a race is unclear, but the self-discovery of Frodo and his three companions is the most important discovery that takes place in the entire novel. To this self-discovery there are many sides. One is the discovery that, unexpectedly and all unwillingly, they have it in them to act heroically when heroism is required. As Elrond puts it after Frodo has volunteered to carry the Ring to its destruction in Mordor, "This is the hour of the Shire-folk, when they arise from their quiet fields to shake the towers and counsels of the great" (I, 284). The major point about the hobbits, and the basis for their success as characters in the book, is their realistic ordinariness—"heroes more praiseworthy than the professionals," Tolkien calls them in a letter.[12] Some quite ordinary folk, Tolkien seems to be saying with the experience of Englishmen in two world wars behind him, rise to desperate occasions. The hobbits are consistently down-to-earth, unpretentious, even insistent in their normality. "I am a hobbit and no more valiant than I am a man, save perhaps now and again by necessity," Pippin asserts (III, 21), while Merry, who has achieved one of the most heroic deeds in the entire war, wakes up from his wound and asks in utterly characteristic fashion: "I am hungry. What is the time?" (III, 145). The contrast between hobbits and a "professional" hero like Aragorn is explicit and important. "We Tooks and Brandybucks," Pippin says to the convalescing Merry, "we can't live long on the heights" (III, 146). In the same spirit, Frodo and Sam perform even more heroic services on their way to destroy the Ring at Mount Doom. Insofar as the book is a story of heroism, it is about the courage of real, ordinary people under pressure. Epic or fairy-tale heroes have their place (I shall have more to say about Aragorn and Faramir below), but we are meant to admire the conscripted hobbits more, and the juxtaposition of the two worlds gives the book its special kind of depth.

The most striking example of heroic humility is Sam, Frodo's servant, who is given stereotypical lower-class speech and seems to know his place only too well. (His full name, Samwise, means "half-wise.") Many readers are offended by both Sam's subservience and his author's undoubted approval of the hierarchical system that requires it. As the story progresses, however, one of the hobbits' major discoveries is that Sam is fully the equal of his more patrician companions and has rightly become, as Frodo describes him to Sam's future wife and in-laws, "one of the most famous people in all the lands" (III, 293). Sam's true stature is acknowledged both in the wide world (where Aragorn, now King of Gondor, bows before him and Frodo) and in the Shire (where he becomes Mayor). In the appendices we learn that after a long and honored life, he is allowed to pass over the sea and rejoin Bilbo and Frodo, the two other Ring-bearers. Social rank is a reality in the world of Tolkien's characters, as in almost all periods of human history; it is not an inevitable destiny.

But the greatest of all the lessons the hobbits learn, and the most important virtue in the story, is pity. Pity runs through the novel from beginning to end. The great teachers of it are Faramir and, above all, Gandalf. "And for me," the latter says of Sauron, "I pity even his slaves" (III, 87). As the four hobbits lose their thoughtlessness and become more experienced, all of them learn pity. Pity for Eowyn gives Merry the courage to strike the Lord of the Nazgul his mortal wound (III, 116). Pity for the ruined steward Denethor, for the wounded Faramir, and for Merry himself is the most important experience in maturing Pippin from the childish scamp he has thus far been. Sam's pity for a black man who has been killed fighting for Sauron is a sign of his own growth ("He wondered what the man's name was and where he came from; and if he was really evil of heart, or what lies or threats had led him on the long march from his home; and if he would not really rather have stayed there in peace . . ." [II, 269]). At the end of the war, home again in the liberated Shire, Frodo looks down at the murdered body of Saruman "with pity and horror" (III, 300). Long before that time, on his journey through the wasteland of Mordor, the increasingly Christlike Frodo has abandoned the wearing of arms and refused to take any part in combat.

The most momentous acts of pity, which allow the Ring to be destroyed and the world to be saved from Sauron's domination, are those that Bilbo, Frodo, and finally Sam extend towards Gollum. At first Frodo is repelled by the thought that Gollum, the hobbitlike creature from whom Bilbo had acquired the Ring

many years earlier, is a creature like himself, and even wishes that
Bilbo had killed him: "What a pity that Bilbo did not stab that vile
creature, when he had a chance!" Gandalf reproves him:

> "Pity? It was Pity that stayed his hand. Pity, and Mercy: not to
> strike without need. And he has been well rewarded, Frodo. Be
> sure that he took so little hurt from the evil, and escaped in the end,
> because he began his ownership of the Ring so. With Pity."
> "I am sorry," said Frodo. "But I am frightened; and I do not feel
> any pity for Gollum."
> "You have not seen him," Gandalf broke in. . . . "I have not much
> hope that Gollum can be cured before he dies, but there is a chance
> of it. And he is bound up with the fate of the Ring. My heart tells
> me that he has some part to play yet, for good or ill, before the end;
> and when that comes, the pity of Bilbo may rule the fate of many—
> yours not least." (I, 68–69)

When Frodo meets Gollum, who has been pursuing him in the
hope of recovering the Ring, he remembers this conversation and
answers the now absent Gandalf: "Very well. . . . But still I am
afraid. And yet, as you see, I will not touch the creature. For now
that I see him, I do pity him" (II, 222).

As Gollum guides Frodo towards the entrances of Mordor, a
strange relationship grows up between them. Frodo comes increasingly under the corrupting power of the Ring; at the same
time, Gollum becomes more hobbitlike. A precarious loyalty
to Frodo nearly overcomes his compulsion to possess the Ring.
At the critical moment, Frodo and Sam are sleeping, ignorant of
the fact that Gollum has betrayed them. When he sees them he
nearly repents.

> A spasm of pain seemed to twist him, and he turned away, peering
> back up towards the pass, shaking his head, as if engaged in some
> interior debate. Then he came back, and slowly putting out a trem-
> bling hand, very cautiously he touched Frodo's knee—but almost
> the touch was a caress. For a fleeting moment, could one of the
> sleepers have seen him, they would have thought that they beheld

an old weary hobbit, shrunken by the years that had carried him far
beyond his time, beyond friends and kin, and the fields and streams
of youth, an old starved pitiable thing. (II, 324)

Sam's jealousy upon awakening drives Gollum to carry out his
betrayal of Frodo, and the moment passes forever. We do not see
him again until the last horrible stage of the quest, when Sam,
like St. Christopher, is carrying Frodo up Mount Doom. When
Gollum attacks them and Sam overcomes him, it is Sam's opportunity to show pity: ". . . he could not strike this thing lying in
the dust, forlorn, ruinous, utterly wretched. He himself, though
only for a little while, had borne the Ring, and now dimly he
guessed the agony of Gollum's shrivelled mind and body, enslaved
to that Ring, unable to find peace or relief ever in life again" (III,
222). The result is that when Sam reaches the Cracks of Doom,
he sees two creatures, both corrupted, fighting for the Ring.
Frodo's likeness to Gollum, often hinted at, has become for the
moment complete. At the climax of the novel, Gollum bites off
Frodo's finger, recaptures the Ring, and falls with it into the
Cracks. Gollum and the Ring are destroyed; Frodo and the world
are saved. "But for him, Sam, I could not have destroyed the
Ring," Frodo says. "The Quest would have been in vain, even at
the bitter end. So let us forgive him!" (III, 225). Pity has brought
about the victory that heroism, whether of hobbits or of the men
who lead the armies of the West, was powerless to win.

Having achieved their several kinds of victories and been duly
honored, the hobbits set out for home. The liberation of the Shire
causes them little difficulty; as Gandalf tells them, "that is what
you have been trained for." At the same time, he informs them,
"You are grown up now," a more ambiguous tribute (III, 275).
The Shire is a land of childhood peopled by children, and those
who have grown up in the wide world find it difficult ever to feel
at home there again. To Frodo, who has grown and suffered the
most, the return "feels more like falling asleep again" (III, 276).
After less than two years at home, he sets out for the Grey Havens

and, together with Bilbo, Gandalf, and the greatest of the Elves, leaves Middle-earth forever. The book proper ends with Sam's return to the claims of domestic life in the Shire; but the design of the work implies that Frodo's companions have outgrown their old home, and in the appendices we find that all three of them move away before their deaths—Merry and Pippin to Gondor, Sam to the Grey Havens and over the sea. Childhood is all very well, Tolkien seems to be saying, and children are worth many sacrifices to protect; but there is something fatally limited about people who remain children forever.

ALTHOUGH HOBBITS are central to the plot of *Lord of the Rings*, human beings are at the center of its meaning. "The Third Age of the world is ended, and the new age is begun," Gandalf tells Aragorn. "And all the lands that you see, and those that lie round about them, shall be dwellings of Men. For the time comes of the Dominion of Men . . ." (III, 249). The age of men is history as we know it. Everything that went before is, in Tolkien's terms, prehistory or myth. In history—we might equally say in adult consciousness—all other "speaking peoples" gradually disappear, leaving humans to their own devices and to what Loren Eiseley called "the long loneliness" of being able to communicate only with their own kind. The responsibilities and spiritual dangers of a human species cut off from all conversation with other creatures are among Tolkien's major concerns. No doubt they were one motive for creating literary works that present a variety of (necessarily fictional) nonhuman perspectives on the world. Hence the nostalgia that infuses those passages of the book that have to do with Elves and Ents. The primeval forests themselves will fall before men. "The New Age begins," Gandalf explains to Treebeard, "and in this age it may well prove that the kingdoms of Men shall outlast you . . ." (III, 258). Even before the destruction of the Ring, it is clear to Elves and Dwarves that their time is coming to an end. Legolas and Gimli discuss the ambiguous future in Minas Tirith:

> "It is ever so with the things that Men begin: there is a frost in Spring, or a blight in Summer, and they fail of their promise."
>
> "Yet seldom do they fail of their seed," said Legolas. "And that will lie in the dust and rot to spring up again in times and places unlooked-for. The deeds of Men will outlast us, Gimli."
>
> "And yet come to naught in the end but might-have-beens, I guess," said the Dwarf.
>
> "To that the Elves know not the answer," said Legolas. (III, 149)

As the mythical allies fade in the light of history, so do the mythical enemies who play such a conspicuous part in the War of the Ring. The future wars of men will be waged against other men, as is already partly the case in Tolkien's novel. Similarly, many of the struggles that are given external shape in myth will become internal, psychological conflicts in historical man and the kinds of literature that go with a historical attitude towards the world. Because two of the most persistent criticisms of *Lord of the Rings* have to do with the use of imaginary monsters as enemies (why, if pity is the central virtue, create enemies like Orcs who cannot be pitied?) and the flatness of human characterization that comes from externalizing all conflict, it is time to look at Tolkien's approach to his human characters. Are they really one-dimensional figures who duel with equally flat adversaries in a simpleminded war of white against black? Or is Tolkien trying (with whatever degree of success) to do something rather more subtle and complicated?

Clearly Tolkien intends his human characters to be varied and differentiated, both as nations and as individuals. Faramir is not Aragorn or Eomer, even though all three are "heroes." Likewise Rohan is not Gondor. The variety that freedom allows to humans and other living creatures is the social counterpart of pity towards individuals. Furthermore, Aragorn, the dominant human char-

101

acter, is more credibly developed than critics often notice. He is a moral archetype, but not *only* an archetype. As a pretender to a vanished throne whose claims no one yet recognizes, "Strider" is defensive and bitter when the hobbits first encounter him. "I hoped you would take to me for my own sake," he tells them. "But there, I believe my looks are against me" (I, 183). "Little do I resemble the figures of Elendil and Isildur as they stand carven in their majesty in the halls of Denethor," he says apologetically to Boromir (I, 261), and his defensiveness does not wholly disappear even when he has become king. "It is a long way, is it not, from Bree," he says to Sam in his moment of triumph, "where you did not like the look of me?" (III, 232). As a combination of Robin Hood and Sherlock Holmes (see I, 201), he is engaging and sometimes amusing. Inevitably he grows more remote and less interesting as he comes into his own as hero and king.

It is perhaps in making this development clear, and more generally in conveying the dignity of Gondor, that Tolkien's style most shows its limitations. As the passages quoted earlier demonstrate, Tolkien is at his best when writing about hobbits; even in describing their apotheoses on the Pelennor Fields or Mount Doom, his style is natural, vivid, and idiomatic. When he tries to show men being noble and heroic, he usually gives way to bombast or archaism.[13] Here is how Aragorn announces himself to Eomer on their first meeting: "'Elendil!' he cried. 'I am Aragorn son of Arathorn, and am called Elessar, the Elfstone, Dúnadan, the heir of Isildur Elendil's son of Gondor. Here is the Sword that was Broken and is forged again! Will you aid me or thwart me? Choose swiftly!'" (II, 36). There is far too much of this sort of pomposity, both in dialogue and in the narration, and it increases as the book goes along. No wonder Aragorn is so often dismissed as a shallow fairy-tale hero whose only function is to be King of the Good Guys.

"How shall a man judge what to do in such times?" Eomer asks Aragorn in the same scene. "As he ever has judged," Aragorn answers. "Good and ill have not changed since yesteryear; nor are they one thing among Elves and Dwarves and another among Men. It is a man's part to discern them, as much in the Golden Wood as in his own house" (II, 40–41). As this didactic passage makes clear, good and evil are objective qualities in *Lord of the Rings*, even though recognizing them in the situations of real life is sometimes as difficult for the characters as it is for real people in the twentieth century. This assumption is shared by all of Tolkien's human characters, but that does not make them characters of unmixed perfection or evil. On the contrary, nearly all of them are mixed, even though the ponderous style sometimes blurs the nature of their inner conflicts. Aragorn makes repeated errors of judgment—"All that I have done today has gone amiss," he complains at one stage (II, 17)—and fails more than once to accomplish his purposes. Boromir and Denethor fight unceasingly against Mordor, yet die corrupted in different ways by the temptations of power. Theoden, king of Rohan, has to be rescued from the illusions of old age before he is ready to join the war. On a less exalted level, the Master of the Houses of Healing is an unbearable pedant but also a dedicated, compassionate healer.

Faramir and Eowyn are the human characters who undergo the deepest sufferings, and in portraying these two Tolkien most effectively combines the performance of heroic deeds with real human qualities. Faramir, the younger son forced to lead his people in war after the death of the favored Boromir, struggles with himself and his harsh father nearly to the point of despair and death. He is described as having "an air of high nobility such as Aragorn at times revealed, less high perhaps, yet also less incalculable and remote . . ." (III, 84). Eowyn, the most fully developed woman in the novel, despairs of her people's future and disguises herself as a man so that she can die in the war. As a warrior, she achieves (together with Merry) the greatest of all feats of arms, the killing of the Lord of the Nazgul; but the conflict with herself and the destiny that has made her a woman in time of war is insoluble through any deed of arms. "Shall I always be left behind when the Riders depart, to mind the house while they win renown, and find food and beds when they return?" she demands of Aragorn, whom she wishes to follow into battle. "All your words are but to say: you are a woman, and your part is in the house. But when the men have died in battle and honour, you have leave to be burned in the house, for the men will need it no more" (III, 57, 58). Later, after she has been wounded, Gandalf explains her despair in similar terms to her brother Eomer: ". . . you had horses, and deeds of arms, and the free fields; but she, born in the body of a maid, had a spirit and courage at least the match of yours. Yet she was doomed to wait upon an old man, whom she loved as a father, and watch him falling into a mean dishonoured dotage; and her part seemed to her more ignoble than that of the staff that he leaned on" (III, 143).

The sensitivity, even feminism, of these passages may seem to be undercut by the fact that once the war is over, Tolkien has Eowyn marry Faramir. "I will be a shieldmaiden no longer," she declares, "nor vie with the great Riders, nor take joy only in the songs of slaying. I will be a healer, and love all things that grow and are not barren" (III, 243). In this passage, however, she restates the central moral virtues that guide the entire novel. Despite the fact that most of the story has to do with warfare, the military virtues are far from being the ones most held up for admiration, whether embodied in women or in men. Boromir, after all, is the most purely warriorlike of heroes, and he fails the moral test early in the book. Faramir, who has been berated by his father for too much "gentleness" in time of war (III, 86), and who has not been tempted by the power of the Ring, is the appropriate mate for Eowyn, as she is for him. "He is bold, more bold than many deem," a soldier tells Pippin; "for in these days men are slow to believe that a captain can be wise and learned in the scrolls of lore and song, as he is, and yet a man of hardihood and swift judgement in the field. But such is Faramir" (III, 39). Like

104

the hobbits, Faramir is a reluctant warrior who does heroic deeds because someone has to protect his country. Gentleness, pity, and learning are the same virtues for humans as for hobbits, and a hero who lacks them is no hero at all. Aragorn himself is recognized as king not by his sword and string of titles but by his "healing hands" and his powers as a "loremaster." Appropriately, the symbol of the new age is not a sword drawn from a stone but a sapling drawn from stony earth by the new king.

If human nature is mixed and complicated, and pity an essential virtue, it is impossible to use human beings as the main enemy in a fictional war where the issues are clearly drawn in moral terms. That would require an intolerance and fanaticism completely foreign to Tolkien's purposes as we have seen them. If the worst evils—slavery, cruelty, the destruction of living things for the mere sake of destruction, the insatiable wish to dominate for the sake of domination—are to be given pure form in fiction, they can be represented only by monsters, and the work in which they appear must be clearly set in a secondary world that is not the real world. Like the *Beowulf* poet, Tolkien has chosen to write such a work, and he takes great pains to differentiate between his monsters and the human beings who sometimes act in their service. The origin of Orcs, the foot soldiers of the enemy, is left mysterious; Treebeard thinks that Sauron created them as a parody of Elves (II, 89), while Frodo believes that he did not create but only corrupted them (III, 190). The Nazgul, as we have seen, were originally men but have long since become quasi-supernatural figures bent to the service of Mordor. Sauron himself is not so much a character (he is never seen) as a name, an oppressive darkness, a lidless eye. His evil lies in a superlative excess of the self-absorption we have seen in hobbits and other peoples: he not only conceives of himself as the center of the world, but wages war to make everyone else recognize his claim.

The victory of Sauron (like, let us say, the triumph of a superhuman Hitler or Stalin) would be a catastrophe for all free peoples. Yet Tolkien is not so naive in the framing of his story as to suggest that the defeat of Sauron solves all problems, or means the end of evil. The world contains an almost endless diversity of creatures, as the hobbits have discovered. Evil is not the result of a conspiracy and derives from no single source. Contrary to what some critics have claimed, *Lord of the Rings* has little relation to "Western ideologies of Cold War."[14] Old Man Willow, the mountain Caradhras, the balrog of Moria, and Shelob (opposite and counterpart of the Elf-queen Galadriel) are all malevolent forces that have no allegiance to Sauron. The complexity of the world is a good thing, but it also means that no victory—for freedom, pity, or the continued flowering of trees—is final. "Other evils there are that may come," as Gandalf explains it; "for Sauron is himself but a servant or emissary. Yet it is not our part to master all the tides of the world, but to do what is in us for the succour of those years wherein we are set . . ." (III, 155). History, once it gets under way, is an ambiguous business.

Lord of the Rings bears some instructive resemblances to another novel of good and evil that was completed in 1949, George Orwell's *1984*. In both stories, an unheroic protagonist carries on a hopeless struggle against the terror and oppression of a dictator so remote from normal life that he seems more a symbol than a reality to his own society. Both dictators maintain their power through virtually supernatural methods of surveillance. In both books, the hero breaks down at the final test. Both authors are obsessed with the relations among language, freedom, and morality. And both find such hope as there is in the least informed, most childish and ordinary element of the population. Tolkien's hobbits and Orwell's proles are simultaneously strong and weak for the same reason: their loyalties are entirely personal and almost never capable of being generalized for either good or evil ends. Although Tolkien's story is set in a remote, unspecified past and Orwell's in what was then the near future, both have the quality of myth—Tolkien's more explicitly, since while Middle-earth is in some sense northwestern Europe, its inhabitants are clearly not part of our world. Its implications are therefore more indirect than those of Orwell's story, but no less real and insistent.

Of the many differences between the two novels, the most revealing has to do with the moral and historical subjectivism with which Orwell's protagonist, Winston Smith, has to contend. This subjectivism is the basis of the Party's domination, and against it Winston is ultimately powerless. How, if the past has no actual or recoverable existence, can anyone compare the relative freedom of an earlier society with the absolute oppression of 1984? Even more important, why should anyone bother to take the risks of combatting a Hitler, a Big Brother, a Sauron, if right and wrong are merely questions of taste and custom? Ethical relativism, when raised to the level of doctrine, has deeply conservative implications. Only the belief that moral values such as freedom and justice have some permanent validity (whether rational or supernatural) gives anyone the opportunity to denounce slavery as evil. This opportunity, which Tolkien's characters possess, is denied to the citizens of Oceania, and its absence is the central issue in Winston's interrogation by the Thought Police. "Is it your opinion, Winston, that the past has real existence?" the inquisitor O'Brien asks superciliously. "Reality exists in the human mind, and nowhere else. . . . You must get rid of those nineteenth-century ideas about the laws of nature. We make the laws of nature."[15] As Tzvetan Todorov points out, drawing an analogy between the Party and some contemporary schools of literary criticism, "To claim that there is no difference between facts and interpretations (in other words that 'everything is interpretation') is to consider force ('the carrot and the stick') as the only way of imposing one's views. . . . it is impossible (without being inconsistent) to defend human rights out of one side of your mouth while deconstructing the idea of humanity out of the other."[16]

If Tolkien ever read *1984*, he left no record of his impressions.

(Orwell was dead by the time *Lord of the Rings* was finally published.) Yet his mind and Orwell's were working along similar lines. The sense of a real past that they inherit gives his characters both moral strength and a sense of responsibility to the other inhabitants, living and dead, of the world they live in, just as the expunging of the past fatally weakens the opponents of Big Brother. The paradox that the elaborate history to which Tolkien's characters are heir is altogether fictional has a central place in our understanding of *Lord of the Rings,* and even in the minds of the main characters. On the borders of Mordor, Sam reflects on the nature of the stories that endure: "Folk seem to have been just landed in them, usually—their paths were laid that way, as you put it. But I expect they had lots of chances, like us, of turning back, only they didn't. And if they had, we shouldn't know, because they'd have been forgotten. We hear about those as just went on. . . . I wonder what sort of tale we've fallen into?" To which Frodo answers: "I wonder. . . . But I don't know. And that's the way of a real tale. Take any one that you're fond of. You may know, or guess, what kind of a tale it is, happy-ending or sad-ending, but the people in it don't know. And you don't want them to" (II, 321).

The design, Tolkien keeps reminding us through passages like this one, is larger than any of the characters realize and involves the creation of a past that sheds light on our present by its very artificiality. Because Orwell's *1984* is set in the primary world, its prophetic power can be (and to some extent has been) diminished by events that fail to happen. *Lord of the Rings* is immune to that kind of falsification, for one of its themes is the transformation of events into story, the truth of which has nothing to do with historical facts. Not only do most of the characters belong to fictional species, but the victory they win with unspecified supernatural help is impossible in the world we know. Because Tolkien's story is a myth, his characters can fight against an adversary of almost unvanquishable strength and yet avoid the fate that Gandalf describes as having to "know as we die that no new age shall be" (III, 156). ("If you want a picture of the future," O'Brien says to Winston Smith in his more circumscribed fictional world, "imagine a boot stamping on a human face—forever."[17])

Shortly before *The Return of the King* was published, Tolkien wrote to W. H. Auden of himself as a man "whose instinct is to cloak such self-knowledge as he has, and such criticisms of life as he knows it, under mythical and legendary dress. . . ."[18] That instinct served him well; for while *Lord of the Rings* is stylistically too uneven to be ranked among the greatest novels, its extraordinary power as a narrative criticism of life comes from its author's careful creation of a secondary world whose separateness from the world of experience is pointed out at every turn, and yet which intersects reality again and again. As usual, the connection is drawn by a character in the book itself. "Do we walk in legends," asks one of the Rohirrim when he first hears about hobbits, "or on the green earth in the daylight?" "A man may do both," answers Aragorn. "For not we but those who come after will make the legends of our time. The green earth, say you? That is a mighty matter of legend, though you tread it under the light of day!" (II, 37). Aragorn's response illuminates not only the purposes of *Lord of the Rings* but those of imaginative literature in general.

6. Robert Frost's Marriage Group

ROBERT FROST has always been the odd man out in twentieth-century poetry. To the influential critical generation that cut its teeth on *The Waste Land,* he seemed technically antiquated, intellectually simple to the point of naiveté, a survivor of the nineteenth century whom the modernist revolution in poetic practice and theory had swept by almost as soon as he began to publish. Worse still, his poems often violated the New Critical commandment against moral and social didacticism by making statements that were clearly intended to apply to the real world. Sometimes, although not usually, they were even preachy. And worst of all, he had a suspiciously large popular audience, of which he was excessively proud.

Warned by memories of Longfellow and Edgar Guest, most critics of any substance assumed that—in our age, at least—a popular poet must be a shallow one. Yvor Winters, in a slashing attack on Frost in 1948, only slightly exaggerated widespread critical opinion by declaring, "His weakness is commonly mistaken for wisdom, his vague and sentimental feeling for profound emotion, as his reputation and the public honors accorded him plainly testify."[1] Not only was he not "modern," but he clearly exploited the public willingness to see him as a red-cheeked, flannel-shirted reinforcer of the small-town pieties, a philosopher who might have stepped off a Norman Rockwell calendar. Had his

defenders (who included Robert Graves and, latterly, Lionel Tril-
ling) been able to point to a single masterpiece that could be
weighed against the other masterpieces of twentieth-century poetry, or even a clear line of growth in what eventually became one
of the longest careers in literary history, the critical verdict might
have been more favorable. But there was no single great poem, no
easily visible line of development, merely sixty-five years of continuous production on more or less the same themes, in more or
less the same style. The result, as Karl Miller put it in the *New York
Review of Books* (10 November 1977), has been that "for all his
medals, prizes, honorary degrees, and visiting professorships, the
universities have not been anything like as eager to study him as
they have been to study Pound, Eliot, and Stevens."

Now that the modernist revolution belongs to a remote period
of history and seems less revolutionary than it once did, perhaps
we can begin to see the limitations of this judgment. The recon-
sideration of Frost's reputation has been proceeding apace for the
last few years, prompted in part by the publication of Lawrance
Thompson's three-volume life and marked most notably, so far,
by Richard Poirier's critical defense, *Robert Frost: The Work of
Knowing* (1977), and William Pritchard's 1984 literary biography.
The styles of *The Waste Land* or *The Cantos* no longer bowl us over
by being new, and the fact that Frost's technique is more recognizably continuous with the poetry of the past is merely a fact
about it, not an indictment. Nor does Frost's lack of interest in the
urban setting of so many modernist works date him as much as it
once seemed to do; the city life described by Pound and Eliot now
seems more quaint, more utterly vanished from the earth, than
the rocky countrysides in which most of Frost's characters live out
their days. The primacy of the metropolis is more doubtful than
it was half a century ago, and we are therefore able to see not
merely that Frost's settings are no more constricting than Eliot's,
but even more important, that his major poems are not *about* nature or rural life any more than Eliot's are about Boston, London,

or East Coker. Their themes and characters transcend the settings in which they are embodied. Furthermore, there is development from volume to volume, a fact which only a critical obsession with technical innovation prevented more readers from seeing until recently.

One of the universal themes which most engaged Frost, about which he had a rich variety of things to say and show, and which reached a clear resolution in two of his most impressive poems, is marriage. Himself one victim of an often tempestuous and conflict-ridden union, Frost in early career set up two opposed images of marriage: those two-person societies in which the differences between men and women lead to bitter misunderstanding and unhappiness; and, in contrast, ideal unions in which the very differences between men's and women's ways of perceiving the world become a source of love and of shared humor. These poems, taken together, add up to a "marriage group" that is at least comparable, in the depth and breadth of Frost's poetic exploration, to Chaucer's linked poems about marriage in *The Canterbury Tales*.

Indeed, in the five volumes Frost published between 1913 and 1928, marriage, unhappy or ideal, is one of the most persistent subjects, with the natural background usually presented either as an Eden for the happy couples or a purgatory for the unhappy ones. Like Chaucer's, Frost's treatment of marriage seems random at first but resolves itself—more or less—into a pattern of development on closer inspection. Generally speaking, poems of conflict give way to those of harmony, celebration, and a sense of oneness with the natural landscape and its inhabitants that is the reward of love, and that is rare elsewhere in Frost's poetry. After *West-Running Brook* (1928), with such sacramental poems as "West-Running Brook," "Two Look at Two," and the more fantastic "Paul's Wife" behind him, Frost seldom returns to the subject of marriage, although there are a number of love lyrics in his later work. The one major exception is "The Subverted Flower" (1942), about which I shall have more to say.[2]

THE PATTERN of anxiety-ridden, blighted marriages is set by "Love and a Question," one of the few poems from Frost's first volume, *A Boy's Will* (1913), that have found their way into recent anthologies. Here a Stranger, who represents the cares and troubles of the outside world, appears at the door of a new-married couple and asks for shelter. The bridegroom cannot decide whether to admit him, for naturally enough his thought is only of his bride. His anxiety goes beyond the inevitable desire to be alone with her, however, for we are told that at the sight of the Stranger, he "wished her heart in a case of gold / And pinned with a silver pin." The poem ends with the bridegroom ominously troubled, uncertain about what to do:

> But whether or not a man was asked
> To mar the love of two
> By harboring woe in the bridal house,
> The bridegroom wished he knew.

These anxieties will be echoed by more than one later Frostian bridegroom.

It is in *North of Boston* (1914) and *Mountain Interval* (1916) that marital conflict and misunderstanding are most fully explored. In such poems as "Home Burial," "The Fear," and "The Hill Wife," Frost treats the loneliness and hysteria of women who, finding their husbands unexpectedly alien, are crushed by solitude. Their environment in these poems is also alien to them, a brooding wilderness that isolates them from the social contacts they so desperately want. That nature does *not* seem so alien to their husbands is one more source of misunderstanding and hostility. In "Home Burial," for example, the lonely farm on which the couple live has become an emblem of death to the wife since the death of her firstborn child. For her hardier husband it remains the familiar field of action, of both life and death, a fact which further causes her to see him as an enemy. The occasion of the poem, revealingly enough, is his attempt to see what she sees from a window—the spot in the family graveyard where the child is buried. Not only does she refuse him any help, she resents his eventual understanding. "Can't a man speak of his own child he's lost?" he asks her, baffled. "Not you!" she answers witheringly. "I don't know rightly whether any man can."

The man's answer to this somewhat daunting response is typically conciliatory; Frost's husbands are usually eager to understand and help their wives, even though their own obtuseness and the hostility of the suffering women often frustrate their good intentions. In this case, when the wife refuses to help her husband help her, he declares:

> My words are nearly always an offense.
> I don't know how to speak of anything
> So as to please you. But I might be taught,
> I should suppose. I can't say I see how.
> A man must partly give up being a man
> With womenfolk.

Such is the frequent complaint of the Frostian husband. Faced with his wife's intention of going off to share her grief with a woman friend, he begs her not to leave; this is a problem for them to overcome together.

The source of her hostility, it becomes clear, is a disastrous misinterpretation: his masculine expression of grief for the child had looked to her like no grief at all.

> I saw you from that very window there,
> Making the gravel leap and leap in air,
> Leap up, like that, like that, and land so lightly
> And roll back down the mound beside the hole.
> I thought, Who is that man? I didn't know you.

At this point the husband despairs of ever being understood: "I shall laugh the worst laugh I ever laughed. / I'm cursed. God, if I don't believe I'm cursed."

The wife's introverted sensitivity, however, is too great, her hurt too deep, to be reached by her husband's more robust sensibility. Rejecting his concern, she declares bitterly:

> You *couldn't* care! The nearest friends can go
> With anyone to death, comes so far short
> They might as well not try to go at all.
> . . . .
> But the world's evil. I won't have grief so
> If I can change it. Oh, I won't, I won't!

But the misunderstanding is not all on one side. Having gotten her to speak her mind, the husband now makes a fatal blunder:

> There, you have said it all and you feel better.
> You won't go now. You're crying. Close the door.

At this she turns to flee from the house, leaving him to bluster and threaten at the opening door. "I'll follow and bring you back by force. I *will!*—" is the hopelessly inadequate response that ends the poem and, presumably, any hope of mutual understanding.

I have examined "Home Burial" in detail because here the pattern of misunderstanding, of the drastically different responses of men and women to the world, is revealed almost paradigmatically. According to Lawrance Thompson, Frost found the poem too painful ever to read aloud. "The Hill Wife," published in the 1916 volume, shows an even greater gap in communication, a husband who is even less capable of mitigating his wife's loneliness and solitude in the natural world. In the first of the poem's five sections, she declares—in one tortuous sentence that conveys near-hysteria—that there is something badly wrong when people "care / So much as you and I" about the annual departure and return of birds, who, after all, care nothing for people. Her sensitivity is even rawer than that of the wife in "Home Burial"; the sight of a beggar at their door makes her intolerably anxious, and she has nightmares about the pine tree outside their bedroom window:

> It never had been inside the room,
> And only one of the two
> Was afraid in an oft-repeated dream
> Of what the tree might do.

Throughout the poem her husband never speaks, and as she follows him silently about the farm in his round of daily tasks, madness or suicide comes to seem the inevitable resolution. Instead, she embraces what terrifies her—whether sanely or madly, and with what ultimate result, neither the husband nor the reader ever knows—and disappears into the wilderness. ("Sudden and swift and light as that / The ties gave. . . .") Here noncommunication has gone as far as it can. In such an extreme case as this, the sensibilities of men and women are simply too different to be bound together; divorce in one form or another is inevitable. Neither has anything of importance to offer the other; indeed, except for the wife's monologue in the first section of the poem, neither spouse addresses a word to the other. Isolation is complete.

IT WOULD BE possible to go through a number of other poems written during this period of Frost's career—"The Fear," "Two Witches," and "A Servant to Servants" are obvious examples—that illustrate other troubled marriages, other powerless husbands and bitterly dissatisfied or hysterical wives. An opposite vision of marriage also makes its appearance in *North of Boston*, however, and becomes increasingly prominent in subsequent volumes. These are the strong and satisfied couples, the ones whose frequent misunderstandings lead only to teasing, never disaster, and whose attitude to life and nature is (in the words of the wife in "In the Home Stretch"), "Dumped down in paradise we are and happy." The happy couples, like the unhappy ones, are usually dominated by the wife's state of mind rather than by the husband's; the greater sensitivity that might have become hysteria in a weaker person here makes possible a wisdom which few of Frost's men achieve. Typically, the fortunate husband is an intellectual theorist, a slightly impractical philosopher, while the wife is serene and utterly down-to-earth. Instead of leading to catastrophe, however, these differences are celebrated by each partner, and the husband does not object to the fact that his wife always has the last word.

The courtship of such a couple is dramatized in "The Generations of Men" (1914), a poem that has been surprisingly neglected by critics and anthologists. In it, Frost's singular ability to reconcile the past with the future—to find in traditions that antedate his young characters a strength which underlies their happiness but does not limit their mischievous vitality—is given full play. A governor of New Hampshire, we are casually informed, has tried to increase tourism by inviting all those with ancestral roots in his state to return at a given time. The numerous Stark clan, having located the origins of their line "In an old cellar hole in a byroad," fix a day to reunite at the spot and "try to fathom / The past and get some strangeness out of it." Alas, it rains, and only two descendants of the line appear, a girl and a boy, each provided with a "passport" that shows its bearer's particular branch of the family tree. Their interest in genealogy soon becomes a pretext for their growing interest in each other, but in Frost things are never quite mutually exclusive. The young man suggests:

> "Why not take seats here on the cellar wall
> And dangle feet among the raspberry vines?"
>
> "Under the shelter of the family tree."

"Just so—that ought to be enough protection."

"Not from the rain. I think it's going to rain."

They sit nevertheless and discuss their reasons for having come on such an expedition. When asked what he sees in such a place, the boy announces that he sees a vision of the first mother of the Starks, drinking cider and smoking a pipe. The girl wonders whether she resembles this remote pioneer ancestor, and the boy obliges by answering that she does. Then, after some mutual teasing, he announces that he has begun to hear ancestral voices in the sound of the brook, just as (twentieth-century lad that he is) he used to imagine voices coming out of the noise of a train or the music of a band. The message of the voices is peremptory but unsurprising:

> Call her Nausicaä, and take a timber
> That you shall find lies in the cellar, charred
> Among the raspberries, and hew and shape it
> For a doorsill or other corner piece
> In a new cottage on the ancient spot.
> The life is not yet all gone out of it.
> And come and make your summer dwelling here,
> And perhaps she will come, still unafraid,
> And sit before you in the open door
> With flowers in her lap until they fade,
> But not come in across the sacred sill—

At this point the girl interrupts to wonder (as surely no reader does) "where your oracle is tending. . . . Whose voice / Does it purport to speak in?" The young man announces that it is their ancestress and declaims, this time in dialect:

> "Son, you do as you're told! You take the timber—
> It's as sound as the day when it was cut—
> And begin over—" There, she'd better stop.

The girl, whose fearless mind is undoubtedly made up, announces that she must depart. Immediately the boy is anxious:

> "Where shall we meet again?"
>
> > "Nowhere but here
> Once more before we meet elsewhere."

That they will meet soon at the altar and be one of Frost's happy couples is obvious, as is the girl's domination of the situation. "I let you say all that," she proclaims, amused by her fanciful wooer, and it is she who closes the poem. It is together, however, that they will reinvigorate the traditions toward which they have been so reverently humorous; in their harmony they will bring back the sound of human voices to what is now merely a ruin.

The relationship between love and the human perception of the natural world is shown most strikingly in "Two Look at Two" (1923), where a couple are taking an evening walk up a mountainside. At the approach of night, they stop before "a tumbled wall" that marks the boundary between the part of the landscape that is safely domesticated and the wilder country above. "This is all," they think regretfully, and prepare to turn back. Then a doe appears, unfrightened—"She saw them in their field, they her in hers"—and after gazing at them for a while passes out of view on *her* side of the dividing wall. But there is more: her mate, "an antlered buck of lusty nostril," soon approaches the wall. He and they stare at each other; then he follows the doe out of sight. But the couple have been given a sign, a grace, which very few of Frost's characters receive.

> Two had seen two, whichever side you spoke from.
> "This *must* be all." It was all. Still they stood,
> A great wave from it going over them,
> As if the earth in one unlooked-for favor
> Had made them certain earth returned their love.

It is, of course, "as if." Nature never sends unambiguous messages in Frost's work. Nevertheless, by venturing with their love to the boundary between the human and the nonhuman, with a humility and receptiveness that their own harmony makes possible, they have been shown that nature even at its least humanized is not altogether alien. They have deserved and received a revelation.

In their passivity, the couple in "Two Look at Two" are untypical of Frost's marriages, happy or unhappy. The teasing banter of "The Generations of Men" is more common, and in Frost's most famous poem of marriage, "West-Running Brook" (1928), we seem to see the same couple a few years later. Their relationship with nature is an active one; indeed, in the first lines of the poem the wife gives a name to the brook, the first step in civilizing the wilderness. The crucial link between their marriage and their relation to the countryside is explicit; after naming the brook, she declares:

> We've said we two. Let's change that to we three.
> As you and I are married to each other,
> We'll both be married to the brook. We'll build
> Our bridge across it, and the bridge shall be
> Our arm thrown over it asleep beside it.

When she goes on fancifully to add that the brook is "waving to us with a wave" in acknowledgement of what she has already said, her husband somewhat pedantically corrects her with a natural explanation. She demurs, which precipitates a mock-argument about the differences between men's and women's minds:

> "It wasn't, yet it was. If not to you,
> It was to me—in an annunciation."
>
> "Oh, if you take it off to lady-land,
> As't were the country of the Amazons

120

We men must see you to the confines of
And leave you there, ourselves forbid to enter—
It is your brook! I have no more to say."

In contrast to what happens in poems like "Home Burial,"
however, this recognition of difference is never allowed to reach
the point of conflict; indeed, the perceived differences are what
make a strong marriage possible when each party has enough
confidence in the other not to be defensive. Instead of striking
back at her husband's seemingly patronizing view of feminine intelligence, the wife shrewdly observes that he does indeed have
something more to say. The lines that follow are as fanciful as
anything that she has said; using the wave as an analogy, the husband gives a Bergsonian/Lucretian explanation of nature, love,
and human identity. "Today," she says tactfully, with the amused
admiration that the genuinely practical often feel for the visionary, "will be the day / You said so." No, he protests, today will be
the day she named the brook. The harmony of this gloriously
matched Adam and Eve is deep enough to include and enhance
the natural world around them as the wife, around whom all else
in the poem revolves, pronounces, "Today will be the day of what
we both said."

WHETHER FROST'S POEMS about marriage or anything else are
modern depends, of course, entirely on how one chooses to de-
fine the term. It is unquestionable, however, that his marriage
poems collectively add up to as varied and subtle a treatment of
that universal theme as one can find anywhere in modern poetry.
His portrayals of weak, anxious husbands and bitter, often hysterical wives are more searching, for example, than those of T. S.
Eliot in *The Waste Land,* and it is probably in his poems of unhappy unions that Frost seems most in accord with what other
twentieth-century poets have had to say about the relations between men and women. The oppressive countrysides in which
they find themselves could just as well be urban landscapes;

whether the country or the city is a waste of solitude or a garden of love depends, after all, on the attitudes of the inhabitant rather than on any objective criteria, whether the poet is Frost or Eliot, Auden or Hardy.

Pointing out that "Frost is often at his best when 'home' is at its worst," Poirier goes on to dismiss "West-Running Brook," and by implication other poems about happy couples, as "poetry written for an audience of literary clubs."[3] Not only is this judgment unfair to the poems individually, it also obscures the pattern of development in Frost's poetically embodied attitudes towards marriage. It is odd that Frost's academic defenders have laid so much stress on his more pessimistic poems and so often dismissed happier ones as presumptively shallow. Both Poirier and—surprisingly—Winters criticize "West-Running Brook" and poems like it for being didactic, which seems to be another way of describing the same flaw.

After *West-Running Brook* Frost wrote little about marriage. One of his most searingly painful poems on the subject, however, "The Subverted Flower," did not appear until 1942. As a poem of failed courtship it belongs to an earlier period of Frost's career, and according to Thompson its delayed appearance in the first volume he published after his wife's death is not accidental. Unlike most of the earlier poems, it is neither fully dramatic nor altogether lyrical, but a peculiarly unsettling combination of the two. The girl who is being courted stands idyllically up to her waist "In goldenrod and brake, / Her shining hair displaced." The poem seems to begin immediately after the man has made a proposal of marriage, or at least an avowal of love. The girl draws back in instinctive repulsion. Lashing his palm with a flower, horribly embarrassed, he attempts to lighten the situation with a half-serious joke: "It is this that had the power." But she does not smile; "either blind / Or willfully unkind," she reduces him to a cringing animal by her lack of positive response. He tries once more:

"If this has come to us
And not to me alone—"
So she thought she heard him say;
Though with every word he spoke
His lips were sucked and blown
And the effort made him choke
Like a tiger at a bone.

She will not help him; indeed, she seems to fear that he will attack her. At this moment her mother calls "From inside the garden wall"—and the gap between her narcissistic purity and the man's shame becomes unbridgeable. The fault is hers for reducing him to a spurned animal:

A girl could only see
That a flower had marred a man,
But what she could not see
Was that the flower might be
Other than base and fetid

. . . .

And what the flower began
Her own too meager heart
Had terribly completed.

It is the man rather than his beloved who flees, followed by the "bitter words" of a hysterical girl who is too young to understand love. The poem ends without mitigation of the horror that both feel:

Her mother wiped the foam
From her chin, picked up her comb,
And drew her backward home.

As a complex portrayal of sexuality too early aroused and its devastating effects on both parties, "The Subverted Flower" can stand comparison with any modern poem about the endlessly complicated relations between men and women. It is, along with Frost's other poems about marriage, a powerful rebuttal to his curiously tenacious reputation for being the unsophisticated per-petuator of a simpler era in life and poetry. As his career gradually comes clearly into focus, these poems remind us that it was, after all, Ezra Pound, that shrewd sniffer-out of twentieth-century lit-erary talent, who stood godfather to Frost's earliest fame.

7. Padraic Pearse:
The Revolutionary as Artist

A N IRISHMAN'S IMAGINATION," one of Bernard Shaw's characters says in *John Bull's Other Island*,

> never lets him alone, never convinces him, never satisfies him; but it makes him that he cant face reality nor deal with it nor handle it nor conquer it: he can only sneer at them that do. . . . He cant be intelligently political: he dreams of what the Shan Van Vocht said in ninetyeight. If you want to interest him in Ireland youve got to call the unfortunate island Kathleen ni Hoolihan and pretend shes a little old woman. It saves thinking. It saves working. [1]

One of Shaw's targets here is certainly Yeats, at whose request the play had been written and whose *Cathleen ni Hoolihan* had recently had its run at the Abbey Theatre. From the standpoint of the analytical, political Shaw, Yeats was a perfect example of the Irishman whose imagination had unfitted him to face reality and whose feelings about Ireland were determined not by knowledge and thought but by symbols that had little relevance in the modern world. So far as I know, Yeats wrote no specific answer to Shaw, although the passages in his autobiographies that deal with the opening of *Arms and the Man* in Dublin might be taken as a kind of revenge. Yeats's real rebuttal of Shaw's case is implicit,

125

however, in much of his later poetry and prose. Indeed, his whole mature life expressed the conviction that while imagination does make one less at home in the conventional world, the reality which it reveals is far deeper and more important than someone like Shaw could ever grasp. The very symbols of nationality which Shaw derided had for Yeats a reality of their own that was far more enduring, and in the long run far more powerful, than the decisions of politicians. Cathleen ni Hoolihan, he would have pointed out, had outlasted any number of secretaries of state for Ireland. The realist's vision is too narrow, his understanding too shallow; in the final analysis truth eludes him.

In all of Ireland there cannot have been a man who would have agreed more strongly with Yeats, had he put his position in these terms, than Padraic (Patrick Henry) Pearse. Like Yeats, Pearse was a nationalist and a poet, although on the question of which profession was more important they would certainly have disagreed. Unlike Yeats he was also a Roman Catholic, an ascetic, a strong supporter of the Irish language, the founder of a school, and— oddly enough—a middle-class progressive with a strong sense of democracy and the rights of the urban poor.[2] To the reader who was acquainted only with his journalistic writings, Pearse might have seemed a much more Shavian sort of Irishman than Yeats: down-to-earth, analytical, concerned with facts. And in a sense this impression is correct. For all his romantic nationalism—to which he gave himself far more wholeheartedly than Yeats ever did—he was also a much more realistic and clear-sighted man in the limited sense that he correctly perceived the direction of events in Ireland, understood cause and effect, and as leader of the 1916 Easter Rising acted in a way that was politically decisive. Whether the Irish Republic as eventually achieved bore much resemblance to Pearse's ideal state is a different question.

Pearse has never received his due as a political man of letters; his reputation remains, in literary discussion, that of a warped fanatic, a failed artist, a man who—paradoxically—functions for

Ireland's greatest poet (in such poems as "The Rose Tree," "The Statues," and the play *The Death of Cuchulain*) as a symbol of heroic action but whose intelligence and even sanity are open to the most serious doubt.[3] This combination of views, as I shall try to show, is both unjust and self-contradictory.

Because of the way in which Pearse sacrificed his life it is usual to regard him as a man of one idea who had lost touch with reality. Such a judgment is unfair. Pearse was a man of many ideas who subordinated everything in himself to one goal, an independent Irish republic. That he did not repress other interests is clear from his writings; he simply kept them in their place and did not allow them to deflect him from his course. For this reason it is wrong to suggest that Pearse was a failed poet who became a revolutionary faute de mieux. Unsatisfactory poet he may have been, but he was a revolutionary long before, and his most important poems and plays are part of the struggle for Ireland. Literature was important to him, but Irish independence infinitely more so.

The distinction is important. Despite the theatrical character of Pearse's last days, despite the deliberate choice of death in what he knew to be for the moment a lost cause, I do not think it can be shown that he was out of touch with reality in the ordinary sense of the term. His perception of what was going on, and how the course of events could be affected, turned out to be more accurate than that of almost any other observer, including the two leading Irish writers of his time. Beyond the expectations of others, the amateurish rising that he led did eventually bring about the dream of centuries. In his view the martyrdoms that followed the rising were necessary for the most practical reasons, and the consensus of historians today is that he was right. If it is ever meaningful to say that the life of an artist can itself become a work of art, then it is true of Pearse; in the death he sought he changed his life into the sort of poem he himself had written—highly romantic, heroic, obscure perhaps on first reading but unified by a logic of its own that connects it at many points with the outside world. It was the quality of artistic completeness in Pearse's life that Yeats—who had sought its equivalent in his own life without great success—came to admire and that led him to write poems about a man for whose political fanaticism he had little use.

Pearse's prose reveals a different man from his poetry and plays. It is very good prose—clear, stylish without being fancy, penetrating, sometimes humorous, and quite sane. Most of it, though not all, consists of speeches, pamphlets, and newspaper articles about the fight for independence, largely written between 1913 and 1916. In them we see the almost Shavian Pearse to whom Yeats would not have felt particularly drawn: a man at once too fanatical and too rational for his taste. The following passage, for example, was written a month before the Easter Rising:

> It is foolish to say . . . that hate is barren, that a nation cannot feed itself on hate without peril to its soul, or at least to the sanity and sweetness of its mind, that Davis, who preached love, is a truer leader and guide for Ireland than Mitchel, who preached hate. The answer to this is—first, that love and hate are not mutually antagonistic but mutually complementary; that love connotes hate, hate of the thing that denies or destroys or threatens the thing beloved: that love of good connotes hate of evil, love of truth hate of falsehood, love of freedom hate of oppression; that hate may be as pure and good a thing as love, just as love may be as impure and evil a thing as hate; that hate is no more ineffective and barren than love, both being as necessary to moral sanity and growth as sun and storm are to physical life and growth. . . . Such hate [of the British Empire] is not only a good thing, but is a duty.[4]

Clearly Pearse regarded many of his contemporaries' cultural and cosmopolitan concerns as distractions from the main business of nationalism, which was to free the nation. To him Cuchulain was nothing if not a guide to action. On Christmas Day 1915, in the preface to a political pamphlet, he wrote: "Ghosts are trouble-some things in a house or in a family, as we knew even before Ibsen taught us. There is only one way to appease a ghost. You must do the thing it asks you. The ghosts of a nation sometimes ask very big things; and they must be appeased, whatever the cost."[5] Again and again Pearse expressed the fear that his genera-tion, like the last, would pass away without making an attempt to throw out the English, as the ghosts demanded. That the cost of such an attempt would include bloodshed he never doubted, and one of the least attractive things about him is the complacency with which he accepted the fact.

There is no indication that Shaw ever met Pearse, or even heard of him until after Easter Week. Since Shaw did not live in Ireland and prior to 1916 had little use for Irish nationalism or its sym-bols, it is hardly surprising that they did not know each other, al-though in 1909 Pearse praised the Abbey Theatre for its courage in producing *The Shewing-Up of Blanco Posnet* despite the threat of censorship. With Yeats, the situation was different; not only were they imaginatively closer, but they met several times. In-deed, Pearse described Yeats in 1913 as "the poet who has most finely voiced Irish nationalism in our time."[6] The evident simi-larities hid deeper differences, however. Yeats and Pearse reacted to the same symbols of Ireland, but Pearse gave himself to them in a way that Yeats never did. In speaking at the grave of Wolfe Tone he declared:

> We have come to the holiest place in Ireland; holier to us even than the place where Patrick sleeps in Down. . . . I feel it difficult to speak to you today; difficult to speak in this place. It is as if one had to speak by the graveside of some dear friend, a brother in blood or a well-tried comrade in arms, and to say aloud the things one would rather keep to oneself.[7]

Early in 1916, writing about the soul of Ireland, he expressed himself in a way that Yeats would probably have approved, although once again his response to the symbol was far more oriented towards political action than Yeats's was.

> When I was a child I believed that there was actually a woman called Erin, and had Mr. Yeats' "Kathleen Ni Houlihan" been then written and had I seen it, I should have taken it not as an allegory, but as a representation of a thing that might happen any day in any house. This I no longer believe as a physical possibility, nor can I convince myself that a friend of mine is right in thinking that there is actually a mystical entity which is the soul of Ireland, and which expresses itself through the mind of Ireland. But I believe that there is really a spiritual tradition which is the soul of Ireland, the thing which makes Ireland a living nation, and that there is such a spiritual tradition corresponding to every true nationality.[8]

Finally, after he so far merged life and art as to summon Cuchulain to the General Post Office, Pearse made a permanent conquest of Yeats's imagination and enrolled himself among the ghosts he had served.

When we turn to his "literary" writings we find him more overtly emotional and less capable, so that the result is rarely satisfactory from the artistic standpoint. It is difficult to tell how much of the romantic melancholia and renunciation we find in them is a matter of convention or of Whitman's influence, and how much of it is the real price he paid for seeking martyrdom.

> Why are ye torturing me, O desires of my heart?
> Torturing me and paining me by day and by night?

The nature of the desires is never made plain, and the imagery of the poem is not specific enough for one to guess. Pearse represents himself as a deer pursued by a pack of hounds.

> No satisfying can come to my desires while I live,
> For the satisfaction I desired yesterday is no satisfaction,
> And the hound-pack is the greedier of the satisfaction it has got,—
> And forever I shall not sleep till I sleep in the grave.[9]

It is impossible to know what the hounds represent here, but the emphasis on desires that must be suppressed and the fascination with death are ubiquitous in Pearse's poetry. (Perhaps the latter is not unrelated to the obsession with guns that reveals itself in his prose.) Consider the psalmlike "A Rann I Made," with its sensuous and loving description of death:

> A rann I made within my heart
> To the rider, to the high king,
> A rann I made to my love,
> To the king of kings, ancient death.

> Brighter to me than light of day
> The dark of thy house, tho' black clay;
> Sweeter to me than the music of trumpets
> The quiet of thy house and its eternal silence.

(320)

The lover is death; the house of the beloved is the grave. One would expect Pearse to have addressed a love poem of this sort to Ireland, not to death. It was, however, his death that he thought Ireland demanded, along with the deaths of many others. In another poem, "Renunciation," we again see Pearse quelling his desires in order to achieve the task he has imposed on himself, which is to end in death. The last stanza declares:

> I have turned my face
> To this road before me,
> To the deed that I see
> And the death I shall die.

(325)

Once again, there is the equivalence between the task of freeing Ireland and death: not only as a realistic recognition of probabilities, but also as the cessation of conflict—a peace which would be welcome when it came. That Pearse's struggles were so obviously internal as well as external argues strongly against the picture of him as a monomaniac to whom only one thing was important.

In the most successful of his revolutionary poems, "The Fool," Pearse sees himself in the guise of

> A fool that in all his days hath done never a prudent thing,
> Never hath counted the cost, nor recked if another reaped
> The fruit of his mighty sowing, content to scatter the seed;
> A fool that is unrepentant, and that soon at the end of all
> Shall laugh in his lonely heart as the ripe ears fall to the
>   reaping-hooks
> And the poor are filled that were empty,
> Tho' he go hungry.

(334)

The parallel of ideas here with Yeats's "September 1913" is striking and certainly places Pearse in the tradition of romantic Ireland and its martyrs. Once again he looks forward to death, but this time there is the suggestion that his death will be followed by an apocalyptic upheaval and the righting of wrong. The fool will be justified in the end, the man who does not save but spends all he has; he is right, the solid men of prudence wrong. He is a fool in Christ. (Not for the first or last time in Pearse, Christ is very much at the disposal of the Irish.)

> I have squandered the splendid years:
> Lord, if I had the years I would squander them over again,
> Aye, fling them from me!
> For this I have heard in my heart, that a man shall scatter, not hoard,
> Shall do the deed of to-day, nor take thought of to-morrow's teen,
> Shall not bargain or huxter with God; or was it a jest of Christ's
> And is this my sin before men, to have taken Him at His word?

(335)

The poem is successful because the paradox of the wise fool comes to life with great feeling and is carried out with consistency, although perhaps we would find the effect less powerful if we knew nothing of Pearse's subsequent career and its effects on history.

> O wise men, riddle me this: what if the dream come true?
> What if the dream come true? and if millions unborn shall dwell
> In the house that I shaped in my heart, the noble house of my
>   thought?

(336)

The fascinating thing about Pearse's poetic prophecies is that they had a way of coming true. For him life really did imitate art. By the end of the poem the lonely fool of the first sections has become the voice of his people:

> Ye shall be foolish as I; ye shall scatter, not save;
> Ye shall venture your all, lest ye lose what is more than all;
> Ye shall call for a miracle, taking Christ at His word.
> And for this I will answer.

(336)

Pearse's most considerable literary work is a play called *The Singer*, of which, ironically, the final manuscript was burnt in the publisher's office during Easter Week. (Other copies survived to be subsequently published.) Superficially it is a peasant drama somewhat in the manner of Synge. Taken in connection with Pearse's life and aspirations, however, it is a most revealing piece of work, whose author dramatizes himself and renders more explicitly here than anywhere else the links that existed for him among Ireland, Christ, and death, as well as making explicit what he intended to do with the short time that remained of his life.

The leading figures are MacDara, the Singer; Maire, his mother; Colm, his brother; and Sighle, an orphan girl whom both brothers love and who loves MacDara. The play begins with a dialogue between Maire and Sighle about the love triangle, and here it totters on the verge of real character development. Soon, however,

133

they begin to talk about the coming rebellion, which Maire says confidently "will be very soon." Sighle says:

> I shiver when I think of them all going out to fight. They will go out laughing: I see them with their cheeks flushed and their red lips apart. And then they will lie very still on the hillside. . . . (9)

The response of the mother indicates the general tone of the play: "I am his mother, and I do not grudge him." The young men, it seems, have been stirred up to the point of armed rebellion by the mysterious Singer, a heroic figure with many Christlike traits. Since MacDara, who has been driven from his home by the English for his seditious songs, has already been described in similar terms, it must be obvious to any reader that the two are one; but the characters in the play do not realize this until much later.

Soon Colm comes in from drilling with the other rebels and announces that the word to rise is expected momentarily, and that the Singer himself may be coming. More rebels arrive, and there is more talk of the Singer.

> A poor man of the mountains. Young they say he is, and pale like a man that lived in cities, but with the dress and the speech of a mountainy man; shy in himself and very silent, till he stands up to talk to the people. And then he has the voice of a silver trumpet, and words so beautiful that they make the people cry. And there is terrible anger in him, for all that he is shrinking and gentle. Diarmaid said that in the Joyce country they think it is some great hero that has come back again to lead the people against the Gall, or maybe an angel, or the Son of Mary Himself that has come down on the earth. (16–17)

Thus introduced as poet, hero and Christ-figure, MacDara enters and is greeted with joy. There is more talk of the rising. Then MacDara announces (somewhat like Christ on the way to Jerusalem) that the occasion is not what it seems.

> I have only finished a long journey, and I feel as if I were about to take another long journey. I meant this to be a home-coming, but it

134

seems only like a meeting on the way. . . . [Ellipsis in original.]
When my mother stood up to meet me with her arms stretched out to
me, I thought of Mary meeting her Son on the Dolorous way. (24)

He has a recurrent vision of martyrdom that draws him on, and
he seems to have renounced selfish desire as a preparation for
it, though not without struggle. After a long passage in which
MacDara describes his experiences of exile and suffering, the
news comes that the English have begun to march against the
rebels. The word has not come for the rising, but despite the older
rebels' insistence on waiting, Colm goes out with a few followers.
After a brief farewell to Sighle, MacDara follows, leaving her for a
hopeless cause just as the bridegroom had done in *Cathleen ni
Hoolihan*. A handful of men march against the English. Maire
announces:

> Men of this mountain, my son MacDara is the Singer that has
> quickened the dead years and all the quiet dust! Let the horsemen
> that sleep in Aileach rise up and follow him into the war! Weave
> your winding-sheets, women, for there will be many a noble corpse
> to be waked before the new moon! (42)

The cautious rebels tell MacDara why so few had followed Colm:
they thought it foolish to fight against overwhelming odds. The
answer is in accordance with "The Fool": "And so it is a foolish
thing. Do you want us to be wise?" Colm falls. MacDara, pulling
off his clothes, advances on the English.

> One man can free a people as one Man redeemed the world. I will
> take no pike, I will go into the battle with bare hands. I will stand
> up before the Gall as Christ hung naked before men on the tree!
> (44)

It is obvious that in this little play the Singer is an idealization of
Pearse himself in the role he had chosen. That he did not hesitate
to compare himself with Christ perhaps says more about his conception of Christ than about his own self-image; Christ seems to

135

have been for him primarily a revolutionary friend of the poor and oppressed, or simply the image of the poor and oppressed, and Pearse is quite generous about comparing *other* revolutionaries with Christ. MacDara goes through the same process of renunciation that Pearse had described in "Renunciation" and "Why Do Ye Torture Me," and he has a vision of approaching martyrdom that is clearly Pearse's and is set forth in the most vivid speech of the play:

> I seemed to see myself brought to die before a great crowd that stood cold and silent; and there were some that cursed me in their hearts for having brought death into their houses. Sad dead faces seemed to reproach me. Oh, the wise, sad faces of the dead—and the keening of women rang in my ears. (25)

MacDara, like Pearse, is the unrecognized leader, the martyr who loves death and Ireland equally, the Christ-substitute whose death will free his people, the poet who by sheer force of will achieves apotheosis as a mythical hero.[10]

Pearse is memorable not merely because he had such dreams but because he lived them out, with results fairly close to those he had envisioned. He was sufficiently clear-sighted to see his opportunity and myth-driven enough to seize it and play the role he had long awaited. In the preface to the last of his political pamphlets he wrote, three weeks before Easter 1916, "For my part, I have no more to say." Literature at this point gave way to action— but action with a pronounced artistic and theatrical quality to it. The remaining few weeks of Pearse's life followed with remarkable accuracy the script he had created. The cautious rebels who refused to rise, the cold silent crowd, martyrdom, and after that victory and the myth: no literary success could possibly compete with such an apotheosis in the mind of a man who lived by romantic imagination and to whom the symbols of heroism and nationalism were more real than grey eighteenth-century houses.[11]

One measure of Pearse's literary importance is the way his actions led greater writers to reassess their feelings about Irish nationalism. In 1913 Yeats had thought romantic Ireland dead and gone; as late as April 1916 Shaw berated the nationalists for wanting to make Ireland into a "cabbage garden," independent but prosaic, provincial and insignificant.[12] After Easter Week, Yeats recorded his sense of reviving myth in a series of poems that ended only with his death, while Shaw became for a while caught up in patriotism towards a nation he had gladly left forty years earlier. In a letter to the *Daily News* in May 1916 he announced, "I remain an Irishman and am bound to contradict any implication that I can regard as a traitor any Irishman taken in a fight for Irish independence."[13] In an extraordinary "speech" he wrote for Casement to use in his own defense, he pointed out (as Yeats later made Pearse do in "The Rose Tree") that "The British scaffold . . . is the altar on which the Irish saints have been canonised for centuries."[14] Dublin returned the favor; *John Bull's Other Island* had a successful revival at the Abbey in the autumn of 1916. Thus we come full circle: even Shaw is changed, if not utterly, at least momentarily; in death Pearse helped bring off a reconciliation between nationalist Ireland and the expatriate playwright.

Despite his considerable accomplishments, are the attitudes and behavior of a Pearse worthy to be admired by succeeding generations? A look at Northern Ireland over the last two decades—a situation for which Pearse cannot be held blameless—may lead us to doubt it.[15] Morally, emotionally, esthetically, there was something of the permanent adolescent about him. He represents one of the most effective examples in real life of that nineteenth-century Romantic ideal, the artist-revolutionary. The twentieth century has been given many reasons to feel more soberly towards such figures, as well as towards the nationalism they embody. In situations where literature and political action exert such a powerful influence on each other, we should prefer the authors of both to be less sentimental. Here, if ever, esthetic flaws reveal an ethical shortsightedness with dire consequences for a whole society.

A slightly younger Irish writer, faced with the same pressures of nationalism and religion, advised silence, exile, and cunning, and followed his own counsel from Trieste to Paris to Zurich. We shall see in the next chapter how a patriotic poet in another small occupied Catholic country ultimately took Joyce's road rather than Pearse's and won, like Joyce, major works from the hard choice of exile over hopeless resistance. Probably no such choice was available to Pearse, either as nationalist or as poet. The special kind of intensity that makes martyrs is usually incompatible with the double vision that makes for mature art. It is both wise and just, however, to see such a figure for what he was—neither madman nor frustrated artist, but a complicated, versatile man whom the symbols of nationality aroused to the point where life and art merged and "terrible beauty" was born out of what would otherwise be senseless, even sordid acts of self-destruction.

8. Czeslaw Milosz:
The Exile as Californian

What is poetry which does not save
Nations or people?
. . . .
That I wanted good poetry without knowing it,
That I discovered, late, its salutary aim,
In this and only this I find salvation.

W HEN Czeslaw Milosz, the author of these ambitious lines,
won the Nobel Prize for Literature in 1980, he was almost
entirely unknown in the United States, the country in which he
has made his home for more than twenty-five years. Born in 1911
to a Polish family in Lithuania (a distinction without a difference
in tsarist geography), he left Poland for France at the age of forty,
then accepted a professorship of Slavic literature at the University
of California in 1960. He has lived in Berkeley ever since and has
continued not only to write poetry and fiction in Polish, but to
translate his own verse (sometimes with the help of collaborators)
into English. He has also written several volumes of vivid reminis-
cence and a distinguished history of Polish literature.

Although Milosz has been a well-known poet in Poland since
before the war, it is not entirely surprising that his reputation in

139

this country has remained obscure even since the Nobel Prize brought him briefly to the attention of the press. In 1978 he aptly described himself as "a poet who can be read only in translation and whose poems do not translate well because of many cultural-linguistic allusions in their very texture." There is a striking paradox in what might be called Milosz's distinguished obscurity: the only American citizen whose poetry has ever won the Nobel Prize is a man who declares, "My mother tongue, work in my mother tongue, is for me the most important thing in life"—and whose mother tongue is that of a small nation in Eastern Europe. (It is also true, however, as Irena Slawinska has pointed out, that "English and American poets prevail among Milosz's patrons"— among them Eliot, Blake, Swift, and as we shall see, Whitman.) An erudite, polyglot member of the Eastern European intelligentsia who came to this country as a middle-aged exile, a witness to some of the most lamentable passages of twentieth-century history, he felt bound to warn American readers at the beginning of his *History of Polish Literature* (1969; revised edition, 1983): "Brought up in Poland, I am imbued, for better or for worse, with the historicism typical of many European intellectuals. For the reader who is expecting an eager search for purely aesthetic values, this will not be a good credential. Literature, to me, appears as a series of moments in the life of the species, coagulated into language and, thus, made accessible for reflection by posterity." Padraic Pearse, similarly obsessed with history, might have made the same points, though with less self-protective irony. Admiringly and rather wistfully, Milosz describes his younger contemporary Leszek Kolakowski as "a good example of the return to the mores of the Enlightenment, when a philosopher did not withdraw into an ivory tower but waged war on the creeds of his contemporaries and when the terms philosophy and literature were nearly interchangeable."

Milosz's historicism has imbued virtually all of his prose writings and much of his verse. In his Nobel Prize address (as printed in the *New York Review of Books,* 5 March 1981), he points out that he remained voluntarily in Poland throughout the German occupation and describes himself, not altogether modestly, as being among the twentieth century's "bearers of memory":

> In the minds of modern illiterates . . . who know how to read and write and even teach in schools and at universities, history is present but blurred, in a state of strange confusion. Molière becomes a contemporary of Napoleon, Voltaire a contemporary of Lenin. . . . For the poet of the "other Europe" the events embraced by the name of the Holocaust are a reality, so close in time that he cannot hope to liberate himself from their remembrance unless perhaps by translating the Psalms of David. . . . During the thirty years I have spent abroad I have felt I was more privileged than my Western colleagues, whether writers or teachers of literature, for events both recent and long past took in my mind a sharply delineated, precise form.

Precise form indeed—several of Milosz's most striking poems are about the destruction of the Warsaw ghetto, which he witnessed in 1943. Ignorance of history is not only a popular failing which every American academic can observe in his students (and many of his colleagues); it also infects theories of literature, with results that are far from insignificant:

> There is, it seems, a hidden link between theories of literature as *écriture,* of speech feeding on itself, and the growth of the totalitarian state. In any case, there is no reason why the state should not tolerate an activity that consists of creating "experimental" poems and prose, if these are conceived as autonomous systems of reference, enclosed within their own boundaries. Only if we assume that a poet constantly strives to liberate himself from borrowed styles in search of reality is he dangerous.

To say that this is not a fashionable set of attitudes among American critics today is putting it mildly. The emphasis on poetic truth and the importance of history is calculated to strike most students of contemporary literature in the United States and Western Europe as antiquated, alien, or both. It is hardly surprising that the *New York Times* headlined the Nobel Prize award "Polish Poet in U.S. Gets Nobel in Literature," or that James Atlas commented in the same issue (10 October 1980), "An unlikely Californian, Milosz finds himself nostalgic for 'the feeling of history and the tragic sense it induces.'"

It is no doubt one of the ironies of literary history that the deeply rooted man who announced these positions, whose lack of regard for many contemporary and American habits of mind is manifest, found himself at the age of forty-nine in California, a place world-famous for its rootlessness and lack of interest in the past. The irony does not end here, however, for by coming to terms with what California meant in the light of his previous experience, Milosz has become a significant if largely unknown figure in the literature of his adopted country. His poems since 1960 balance past and present, native and alien life and language. They are the work of a man who has led two lives in radically different times and places and is trying to unite them in thought and art. The result is a major and unique contribution to American literature, one that has gone virtually unnoticed by commentators who have been content to think of Milosz simply as an exile whose career since 1960 has been no more than a prolongation of his earlier life on native soil.

Milosz's first reaction to exile, he explains in "To Raja Rao" (significantly, the only poem in his *Selected Poems*[1] that was written originally in English), was very much what one might expect:

> For years I could not accept
> the place I was in.
> I felt I should be somewhere else.
>
> . . . .
>
> Somewhere else there was a city of real presence,
> of real trees and voices and friendship and love.

142

Exchanging Poland for France and then America was no help; like Solzhenitsyn, although less apocalyptically, he found East and West animated by opposite vices.

> Ill at ease in the tyranny, ill at ease in the republic,
> in the one I longed for freedom, in the other for the end of corruption.

("The decision to refuse all complicity with the tyranny of the East—is this enough to satisfy one's conscience? I do not think so. I have won my freedom; but let me not forget that I stand in daily risk of losing it once more. For in the West one also experiences the pressure to conform—to conform, that is, within a system which is the opposite of the one I escaped from," says Milosz in *The Captive Mind*, published as long ago as 1953.)

There is a subsequent stage in exile, however, at least if the one exiled is fortunate and brave enough. The poem continues:

> I learned at last to say: this is my home,
> here, before the glowing coal of ocean sunsets,
> on the shore which faces the shores of your Asia,
> in a great republic, moderately corrupt.

This stage marks not an end but a new beginning. It does not, needless to say, fully resolve the problems that have been left behind, the guilt and disorientation of the witness to history, the émigré, the survivor in lotus-land. Guilt of this kind is a major theme in the poetry that Milosz has written over the last forty years. He speaks again and again of scenes of horror half-recalled in dreams, of friends and strangers killed by the Gestapo, of various forms of desertion. In many of his poems, the landscape itself is deformed by history into nightmare. As the exiled Russian poet Joseph Brodsky wrote in nominating Milosz for the Neustadt Prize in 1978: "The wasteland he describes in his wartime (and some postwar) poetry is fairly literal: it is not the unresurrected Adonis that is missing here, but concrete millions of his countrymen. . . . Out of these ashes emerged poetry which did not so much sing of outrage and grief as whisper of the guilt of the survivor."

Such poetry remains an important part of Milosz's opus, but it is not the whole story. Because his work is so little known to American readers, I shall be quoting a great deal of it, and something should be said here about the way he chooses to present it in his major English collection. The brief section of *Selected Poems* that contains works written before the war is entitled, with a wistful irony, "How Once He Was." That section is followed by "What Did He Learn," which comprises poems written during and after the German occupation. The last section, including nearly half the poems in the book, is "Shore." As in the poem quoted above, the shore is that of California. It is in "Shore" that the ghosts of Europe are—not exactly exorcised, but made to cast a different shadow in a landscape whose paucity of rooted things bears some relation to the clarity and intensity of its sunlight. The lowering clouds of history may encourage richer vegetation; they also sometimes obscure things that are close at hand.

THE ENGLISH-BOUND reader whose interest in Milosz is as an American poet of European background, rather than a European poet accidentally resident in America, will be delighted to discover rumors of Walt Whitman in a poem entitled "Hymn," written as early as 1934. In the poet's own translation, the most lyrical passage of this youthful work runs:

> Roll on, rivers; raise your hands,
> cities! I, a faithful son of the black earth, shall return
>   to the black earth,
> as if my life had not been,
> as if not my heart, not my blood,
> not my duration
> had created words and songs
> but an unknown, impersonal voice,

only the flapping of waves, only the choir of winds
and the autumnal sway
of the tall trees.

There is no one between you and me
and to me strength is given.

Milosz's admiration for Whitman and the visionary tradition has been an abiding influence, one which naturally reappears in the poems written after he came to this country. In "Album of Dreams," Whitman's name is even mentioned ("With a broad white beard and dressed in velvet, / Walt Whitman was leading dances in a country manor / owned by Swedenborg, Emanuel."). More significantly, "Throughout Our Lands," a long work in which present California and past Lithuania are contrasted in a series of concrete meditations, begins with an invocation of a valued predecessor:

When I pass'd through a populous city
(as Walt Whitman says, in the Polish version)
when I pass'd through a populous city,
for instance near San Francisco harbor, counting gulls,
I thought that between men, women, and children there is
something, neither happiness nor unhappiness.

It would be going too far to say that Milosz finds Whitman an altogether kindred spirit. No skeptical twentieth-century intellectual could possibly make such an affirmation, whatever his background. The following passage from the same poem is both like and unlike Whitman's dream sequences:

Between the moment and the moment I lived through
    much in my sleep
so distinctly that I felt time dissolve
and knew that what was past still is, not was.
And I hope this will be counted somehow in my defense:

145

my regret and great longing once to express
one life, not for my glory, for a different splendor.

The distinction in the last line would have been alien to Whitman, even after his own harrowing encounters with history. Nevertheless, in the tormented dreams, the merging of past and present, the aspiration (however thwarted) towards universal celebration, the similarities run deep.

A California poet whom Milosz has long admired in a more qualified way is Robinson Jeffers. Like Whitman and Milosz, Jeffers yearned for what critical prose can identify only as a mystical sense of the wholeness and saving beauty of reality, a lasting vision of the world's oneness in which all the accidents and terrors of actual life cease to be important. Milosz is drawn towards such a vision even while he remains skeptical of it; Jeffers found its fulfillment, rather precariously, in nature at its most inhuman. For both poets, history is a personal burden. But while Jeffers' solution was to apotheosize predatory hawks, cruel splendor, a rocky coast with few human inhabitants, Milosz finds nature in the raw just as repellant as the mindless atrocities of conquerors. The psychic problem of history has many possible solutions, with varying degrees of satisfactoriness. "To Robinson Jeffers" is Milosz's answer to one of the most seductive. The opening is suitably brusque:

If you have not read the Slavic poets
so much the better. There's nothing there
for a Scotch-Irish wanderer to seek.

The "Slavic poets," as Milosz conceives them here, inhabited a peaceful, anthropocentric landscape where "the sun / was a farmer's ruddy face" and nature a place where humans found themselves (naturally) at home. Jeffers' landscapes, on the contrary, are filled with violence and solitude, the heritage of a northern warrior race that listened too long to the ocean.

146

Czeslaw Milosz

Prayers are not heard. Basalt and granite.
Above them, a bird of prey. The only beauty.

"What have I to do with you?" Milosz asks. To be sure, the Lithuanian landscape was a deception; the way of life it seemed to affirm perished in other sorts of violence. Nevertheless, human values—however fragile—remain at the center of the poet's vision. The inhumanity of Jeffers' God is no more admirable than the inhumanity of historical processes. Perhaps direct experience of the latter is an inoculation against falling in love with the former.

> And yet you did not know what I know. The earth teaches
> More than does the nakedness of elements. No one with
>   impunity
> gives to himself the eyes of a god.
> . . . .
> Better to carve suns and moons on the joints of crosses
> as was done in my district. To birches and firs
> give feminine names. To implore protection
> against the mute and treacherous might
> than to proclaim, as you did, an inhuman thing.

Far from being Eden, the wilderness is simply a void. Civilization with its morality may be a frail creation, but there is no substitute for it. How could there be, for a poet whose mind is filled with such images of nightmare as the following (from "Album of Dreams")?

> They ordered us to pack our things, as the house was
>   to be burned.
> There was time to write a letter, but that letter was with me.
> We laid down our bundles and sat against the wall.
> They looked when we placed a violin on the bundles.
> My little sons did not cry. Gravity and curiosity.
> One of the soldiers brought a can of gasoline. Others
>   were tearing down curtains.

147

The category of experience here is altogether outside Jeffers' awareness, despite his professions of complacency towards the destruction of civilization.

And yet the comparatively historyless California landscape does make a healing difference. Vanished Lithuania and burning Warsaw look different in its light.

> True, when the manzanita is in bloom
> and the bay is clear on spring mornings
> I think reluctantly of the house between the lakes
> and of nets drawn in beneath the Lithuanian sky,

Milosz tells us in "Elegy for N. N." There is a serenity about California that is profoundly appealing. The softer features of the landscape offer a vision of an order that is not human, but at the same time is by no means inimical to the values of civilization. Even basalt cliffs, even birds of prey, may have their place in easing the burdens of history. Here, one feels, is a good place for civilization to flower. If it has not altogether done so, Milosz seems at times to be thinking, neither has tyranny. (The works of humanity are always ambiguous; Berkeley and Hollywood are equally products of California.) There is the sweetness of air (though, alas, neither in Berkeley nor in Hollywood), the clarity of light, the mystery of fog, the grandeur of mountains in the distance—an inviting place even to the unwilling exile; a combination, perhaps, of a Van Gogh painting and a Japanese print, those pictorial legacies of great troubled civilizations. If it is not the fulfillment of history, it is more than lotus-land. So in "Dithyramb":

> We have seen so much on earth and yet malachite mountains
>   at sunset are greeted as always with a song and a
>   low bow.
> The same spring dance summons when under the rubble of
>   basalt cliffs flocks of birds plunge in translucent
>   waters of coves.

And a finny hand of a sea otter glimmers as it wallows
   in the foam at Point Lobos.
While in the fog the red of azaleas glows from the bottom
   of steamy ravines.
Nothing has been added, nothing has been taken away,
   o imperturbable, perfect, inviolable world.
No memory is preserved about anything that would be ours
   for certain.

To be sure, painful memories come back immediately—of childhood, of war, of the remote historical past of Europe. But the
context is different from what it was. It is too much to say that
images of the Golden State overpower the sad past. But they
certainly change it into something richer and more universal.
Looked at this way, the tragedy of Eastern Europe ceases (for the
reader) to be remote and becomes part of the American landscape of imagination, even as (for the writer) something of the
opposite process occurs. For each party, a new relationship is established between two disparate and important experiences, one
alien, the other relatively familiar, in which each element is en-
riched by the other.

California is not as devoid of history as all that, of course; it
only seems so because of the fluidity of life there and because few
of its inhabitants have lived there for more than a generation or
two. One of the ways in which Milosz the poet assimilated himself to his new home was by meditating on its history. It would
have been very surprising if such a writer had rested content with
landscape. In fact he has had more to say about California's past
than most native poets. In "Throughout Our Lands," from which
I have already quoted, he casts his mind back to the first Europeans who lived in the Far West: among them Junipero Serra, the
Franciscan friar who founded the California missions in the eighteenth century. Perhaps Milosz sees (at least playfully) a certain
parallel between his own situation and that of the missionary
who wandered earnestly west from Spain and north from Mexico:

149

Was Father Junipero an alien, when on mule-back
he came here, wandering through the deserts of the south.
He found redskin brothers. Their reason and memory
were dimmed.

The focus soon shifts, however, from the exile to his flock, and
Junipero comes to seem a rather naive bearer of European civilization to barbarians who are probably better off without it. His
message of salvation falls at first on deaf ears ("poor people, they
had lost the gift of concentration"). In fact, it is to the soon-
displaced Indians that Milosz feels a deeper sense of gratitude.
The Indians lacked writing and had primitive tastes.

Nonetheless it was they who in my place took possession
of rocks on which only mute dragons
were basking from the beginning, crawling out of the sea.
They sewed a cloak from the plumage of flickers,
    hummingbirds, and tanagers,
and a brown arm, throwing back the mantle,
    would point to: this.

An earlier explorer than Junipero Serra, Cabeza de Vaca, met
an even less enviable fate among the pre-European inhabitants of
the West. Not a missionary whose journey was deliberate, he was
only an exile who landed from "a boat thrown up on the sand by
surf, / crawling naked on all fours, under the eye of immobile Indians." Alternately worshiped as a long-expected god and punished when his miracles miscarried, he endured a life not altogether dissimilar to that of the European intellectual exile in the
twentieth century. Whether such a parallel was in Milosz's mind it
is impossible to say, but the episode comes at the end of the poem
in which he goes furthest to set up reverberations between the
settler of the past (Indian, missionary, castaway) and himself; between memories of Europe and images of the American West; between simple realities like a pear and the difficulty of naming it
when one has had to live in too many languages. Perhaps the best

150

writing about places is often done by exiles. It is nonetheless surprising, but true, that some of the best poems ever written about
California and the West were composed in Polish.

In "Ars Poetica?" (from *Bells in Winter*), Milosz writes:

> The purpose of poetry is to remind us
> how difficult it is to remain just one person,
> for our house is open, there are no keys in the doors,
> and invisible guests come in and out at will.

For obvious reasons, that difficulty is one of which Milosz has
been unusually aware. In *Native Realm* (1958; English translation,
1968), he wrote, "My own case is enough to verify how much of
an effort it takes to absorb contradictory traditions, norms, and
an overabundance of impressions, and to put them into some
kind of order." The continuing effort to do so, in the second stage
of his exile and at an age when most poets have long ceased to
assimilate new experience into their art, is what gives Milosz
a special claim on American readers. Its success is what most
amply justifies, at least to the reader who has no Polish, his Nobel
Prize.

> The first movement is singing,
> A free voice, filling mountains and valleys.
> The first movement is joy,
> But it is taken away.

So Milosz declared in "The Poor Poet," in the burning Warsaw
of 1944. His "first movement," of course, was life as a young
writer before 1939, sometimes prophesying bad days to come but
living nonetheless in a sort of prehistorical present. The "second
movement" was the war, defeat, what has come to be known as
the Holocaust (which, he reminds us in his Nobel address, was
not restricted to Jews), and then the greater betrayal that followed
the coming of peace. For the first half-decade of Soviet rule,
Milosz chose not to become an exile, just as he had chosen to wit-

ness and resist the German occupation. But of the taking away of joy there was no end, and in 1951 his "second movement" ended in emigration.

It is with the American poems of his "third movement" that I have been mainly concerned, not only because they are the ones most accessible to American readers, but also because in them some of the harshness of history is mitigated, if not quite overcome. In them Milosz finds himself—sometimes—in a present that is no longer haunted, that has room for other things besides memory, even for joy. His passage through the horrors of history to a degree of posthistorical serenity testifies powerfully to the resources of both imagination and poetic art—resources which have been greatly in demand during his lifetime. The successful exercise of such gifts may lead to more important rewards than a Nobel Prize, as "Gift," one of the last pieces in *Selected Poems,* suggests:

> A day so happy.
> Fog lifted early, I worked in the garden.
> Hummingbirds were stopping over honeysuckle flowers.
> There was no thing on earth I wanted to possess.
> I knew no one worth my envying him.
> Whatever evil I had suffered, I forgot.

This time, no painful memories intrude. To be a survivor in this sense is a matter not for guilt but for triumph.

One of the spiritual dangers of exile is that the one exiled may believe his own experiences, his own history, to be the only kind that lead to wisdom. This belief may manifest itself in an arrogant condescension towards those people among whom his exile is spent, a condition as unfavorable to art as the fanaticism of a Pearse. To judge by his poems of exile that have appeared in English, Milosz's art has avoided this fate by remaining open to the possibility of making a new home for itself, without of course forgetting the old one. Three concerns have preoccupied—one might almost say obsessed—Milosz's writings since the war: the value of European civilization, the persistence of history, and the artist's duty to tell the truth, both for his own sake and for the sake of his society. Dwelling on these preoccupations in the benign but alien setting where they seem at first to be drastically out of place; allowing the literal and symbolic extremes of past and present, old Europe and new California, to interpenetrate and illuminate each other; at his frequent best, doing all this with great power and inventiveness—it was these accomplishments that signalled his transformation from a promising young poet of early–twentieth-century Eastern Europe into a major poet of worldwide significance in the late twentieth century.

9. Explorations of America

With a few important exceptions, nationalism as a strongly held attitude is conspicuously absent from modern poetry in English. An overtly nationalistic poem like Drayton's "Ballad of Agincourt" has hardly any parallels in the twentieth century. For a variety of reasons, skepticism about the value and an awareness of the dangers of national self-assertiveness have entered the language and moral attitudes available to modern poets. The cosmopolitanism of the most influential modernists and the disillusionments of the First World War are two obvious sources of this skepticism, but perhaps there are older and deeper ones as well: for example, the fact that English poetry became a transnational enterprise precisely at the time, in the nineteenth century, when modern nationalism was taking shape. An American, Australian, or Canadian who has been educated on British poetic models finds it difficult to use them in the service of national self-assertion without some obvious ironies arising in his mind.

For whatever combination of reasons, highly regarded poetry that is explicitly nationalistic (as opposed to merely patriotic in a general way) has in the twentieth century been restricted on the whole to small or embattled nations in conditions of crisis: Yeats's poems about Irish independence, for example, or Hugh MacDiarmid's about Scotland, or the more nationalistic passages of Eliot's *Four Quartets*. "Highly regarded," of course, raises the possibility that skepticism about nationalism is an attitude of critics rather than of poets, and undoubtedly one could find in the twentieth century a great deal of nationalistic verse that in previous centuries would have been labelled "popular" as opposed to serious or literary poetry. Nonetheless, it is a fact that the major poets of the twentieth century, even Kipling, are far less comfortable asserting nationalistic attitudes in verse than their predecessors from the Renaissance through the eighteenth century. If James Thomson were alive today, he might very well write a series of poems thematically similar to "The Seasons"; it is much less likely that he would write a modern equivalent of "Rule, Britannia."

None of this means that nationality and the exploration of its constituents has not been a major theme in the literature of our time. It has, perhaps all the more so as the differences between one place and another seem to lessen. I am speaking here not of the regionalism that is such a common feature in modern British and American literature, but of national self-definition. Self-definition is an entirely different activity from self-assertion, and an inevitable one in nations that have been created in recent times by settlers whose descendants are often at a loss to know what makes them a nation besides their ancestors' common, willed act of immigration. It is hardly too much to say that this need to create a national identity in the act of understanding it has obsessed the literatures of America and the Commonwealth countries since their beginnings. Much American writing from the seventeenth century onwards has embodied a heroic attempt at national definition, which reached its nineteenth-century peak in the poetry of Whitman. The history of this literary theme—of an Eden settled by Europeans, who overcame the original inhabitants and declared their independent identity by an act of self-creative will—has in turn been traced exhaustively by scholars and critics, and there is neither space nor need to summarize it here.

Since Whitman's time until recently, the literary definition of America has been carried on more conspicuously and effectively by novelists than by poets. The works of Mark Twain, Henry James, F. Scott Fitzgerald, Ernest Hemingway, and William Faulkner are obvious examples, and occasional attempts at this sort of thing in the poems of Robert Frost (for example, "The Gift Outright") and others do not have the same weight. Because the adequate exploration of national identity involves history, characters, and complex attitudes, novelists are at an obvious advantage in a time when the dominant poetic form is the short or "lyric" poem. In *The Place of Poetry* (University Press of Kentucky, 1981) I described the decline of the book-length narrative or meditative poem and gave some reasons for the dominance of the short poem since the middle of the nineteenth century. Since book-length poems that tell a story or expound ideas in detail are precisely the kind best suited to the task we are discussing, we should not be surprised that prose fiction largely appropriated it, along with so many other tasks and themes, once the scale of *Leaves of Grass* had come to seem ungainly or merely impracticable by Whitman's successors.

"Are stories no longer told in poetry?" Dana Gioia asked in the *Kenyon Review* for spring 1983.

> Important ideas no longer discussed at length? The panoply of available genres would seem reduced to a few hardy perennials which poets worked over and over again with dreary regularity— the short lyric, the ode, the familiar verse epistle, perhaps the epigram, and one new-fangled form called the "sequence" which often seemed to be either just a group of short lyrics stuck together or an ode in the process of falling apart.

Gioia discussed some of the advantages of longer forms and then put his finger on an important reason for their decline in the wake of modernism:

The major problem facing the long poem today is that contemporary theory allows the poet almost no middle ground between the concentration of the short lyric and the vast breadth of the epic (the modern epic, that is, in its distinctive form as the historical culture poem). . . . American literature needs a more modest aesthetic of the long poem, a less chauvinistic theory which does not vainly seek the great at the expense of the good and genuine. It needs to free poets from the burden of writing the definitive long poem and allow them to work in more manageable albeit limited genres like satire, comedy, unheroic autobiography, discursive writing, pure narrative—be it fictional or historic. . . .[1]

Drawing attention to the eclipse of a literary form is often a step towards reviving it, and as Frederick Feirstein pointed out in the same issue of the *Kenyon Review,* most of the genres that Gioia called for are again being practiced in a variety of ways. The lyric poem could accommodate some themes and ambitions supremely well and offered many poets a welcome discipline after the verbosity of the most celebrated Victorians. But the very successes of its practitioners, from Hopkins and Yeats through Frost and Eliot to the present, exhausted many of its possibilities in the act of exploiting them. Sooner or later, new poets would wish to escape from the shadow of their immediate predecessors—just as the modernists had done with theirs—by trying themes and forms that had fewer recent associations. One result has been a widespread but mostly unheralded revival of the book-length poem in America during the last decade or so. Another, closely related, has been a return to the theme of national identity in an era which, like Whitman's, makes that identity a matter of obsessive concern. The end of the twentieth century is in most respects a more troubling time than Whitman's, and the identity to be explored is not the same as it was in the first century of the republic. Nonetheless, Whitman, Cooper, Emerson, and their contemporaries would recognize important continuities, if only because searching for the essence of America is such a characteristically American thing to do.

From many poems that might be chosen to illustrate these assertions, I have selected three: Robert Pinsky's *An Explanation of America*, Frederick Feirstein's *Manhattan Carnival*, and Robert Penn Warren's *Chief Joseph of the Nez Perce*.[2] They are a diverse group in their forms, in their settings, in their authors' outlooks on life in general and America in particular; yet they all embody a deep desire to get to the heart of American identity, which in varying ways all three writers (like most Americans since James-town) feel to be unique. None of these poems is an epic; all are ambitious "public" poems. My concern in examining them is not so much to evaluate them as to see how three contemporary poets have experimented with long forms—blank-verse medita-tion, fictional narrative in heroic couplets, and historical narrative in free verse—while exploring a theme of overriding significance. Looked at together, they incarnate three ways of writing a book-length poem today and also three approaches to what might be called, in medieval romance fashion, the Matter of America.

IN *The Situation of Poetry* (1976), Robert Pinsky celebrated the bi-centennial of American independence by calling for a return to the "prose virtues" in poetry. Poetry, he declared, should be as well written, and sometimes as discursive, as good prose. "Color-less and reactionary though such a position may seem," he added, mindful of the recent history of American verse, "it is worth taking up." Then he went on to explain what he had in mind by "prose virtues" and to assert that late–twentieth-century poets might find them to be necessities:

> If the plural is analyzed, the virtues turn out to be a drab, un-glamorous group, including perhaps Clarity, Flexibility, Efficiency, Cohesiveness . . . a puritanical assortment of shrews. They do not as a rule appear in blurbs. And yet when they are courted by those

who understand them—William Carlos Williams and Elizabeth Bishop would be examples—the Prose Virtues are transformed from a supporting chorus to the performers of virtuoso marvels. They can become not merely the poem's minimum requirement, but the poetic essence.[3]

Pinsky's *An Explanation of America* (1979), subtitled in Yeatsian fashion *A Poem to My Daughter*, puts most of those virtues to use in an extended meditation whose discursive purpose is proclaimed by its title.

To explain America poetically, it is necessary first to delineate the person for whom the explanation is intended. The rhetoric of explanation must be ad hominem, in the correct sense of that commonly abused phrase. The daughter for whom the explanation is nominally devised seems hardly the sort of child thought to be typically American; she is imaginative, solitary, infantile in many ways but with the dreams of an adult—"not / A type (the solitary flights at night; / The dreams mature, the spirit infantile) / Which America has always known to prize." She is, in short, an outsider, not a joiner, not likely to be at home with American gregariousness, a potential object of persecution, a disconcertingly intelligent child whose eyes behind their owlish glasses betray "The gaze of liberty and independence / Uneasy in groups and making groups uneasy." Already a note of alienation has been struck between the person to whom the explanation is directed (the explainer himself is not yet an issue) and the thing to be explained. We are a long way from Whitman's uncontradictory sense of America as a unified mass of individualists.

The possibility that America in the fullness of its development has become a less benign creation than Whitman hoped inheres in the daughter's childish forms of alienation. Dream and reality have parted, leaving behind the wake of ambiguities that require the poet's explanation. Thus the first question is what, after the variety and empty vastness of the American continent, to show.

What do I want for you to see? I want—
Beyond the states and corporations, each
Hiding and showing after their kind the forms
Of their atrocities, beyond their power
For evil—the greater evil in ourselves,
And greater images more vast than *Time*.
I want for you to see the things I see
And more, Colonial Diners, Disney, films
Of concentration camps, the napalmed child
Trotting through famous newsfilm in her diaper
And tattered flaps of skin, *Deep Throat*, the rest.

In its content, its emphases, its development, its juxtaposition of the horrific and the banal, this catalogue of American realities is far different from anything in "Song of Myself." Evil and banality infect not only institutions but American selves. Television and Vietnam have both happened. If the New World was ever Eden, the Fall was a long time ago. Democracy, however desirable, has solved few problems (as the daughter puts it, "Voting *is not* fair").

I want our country like a common dream
To be between us in what we want to see—
Not that I want for you to have to see
Atrocity itself, or that its image
Is harmless. I mean the way we need to see
With shared, imperfect memory: the quiet
Of tourists shuffling with their different awes
Through well-kept Rushmore, Chiswick House, or Belsen. . . .

Not discoverers or pioneers, not Columbus or Lewis and Clark, but tourists.

What follows is predictably fragmentary, impressions of a land and history described in the last line of the poem as "So large, and strangely broken, and unforeseen." It is not on the whole an attractive portrait.

The plural-headed Empire, manifold
Beyond my outrage or my admiration,
Is like a prison which I leave to you
(And like a shelter)—where the people vote,
And where the threats of riot and oppression
Inspire the inmates as they whittle, scribble,
Jockey for places in the choir, or smile
Passing out books on weekdays.

An empire is characterized, in Pinsky's terms, by variety, mobility, and above all power. Americans move around so much that regional differences, indeed all sense of place, become themselves "a kind of motion." An image, drawn from Willa Cather, of unmotivated suicide in the endless prairies of the Middle West suggests the aimlessness of so much American mobility, which is perhaps little more at bottom than a love of death. In a nation whose inhabitants have to create it imaginatively out of such a vast emptiness, a lasting individual or corporate identity is hard to come by. No wonder the official symbol of the United States, the eagle who represents flight and power, is a "wild bird with its hardware in its claws."

What Whitman would have made of America a century after his death is anybody's guess, but he would almost certainly have resisted the notion that classical European parallels could offer useful insights. For him and his followers, America was unique in the world's history, subject to few of the limitations that affected other empires. Pinsky, however, follows many twentieth-century historians and political commentators in seeing close parallels between America and Rome, frugal republics that begat decadent empires. The center of his poem is a free translation from a letter in which Horace reflected on private versus public life in an imperial society. *Public* and *private* mean different things in an empire from what they meant in a small republic, Roman or American. For Pinsky's Horace, a detached retirement is the only way to lead a life that is both free and dignified. A public life in which those virtues can be maintained has become, if not absolutely impossible, at least very difficult. What can traditional civic virtues mean in such a civilization? At bottom, the willingness to commit suicide rather than submit to tyranny is the only solid basis for liberty—a liberty which only detached individuals can possess, not one that undergirds the whole social structure. The republic is gone forever; only in the isolated, detached self of the stoic does anything of its spirit survive.

Republics liberate, empire imprisons. Thomas Jefferson on his mountaintop at Monticello represented an altogether different classicism from Horace at his Sabine farm. A third civic possibility is Brutus. Pinsky finds it hard to decide what kind of fortune to wish for a daughter who must live in an age of Caesarism. Whatever one's talents, to be a Jefferson is now impossible.

> Since aspirations need not (some say, should not)
> Be likely, should I wish for you to be
> A hero, like Brutus—who at the finish-line
> Declared himself to be a happy man?
> Or is the right wish health, the just proportion
> Of sun, the acorns and cold pure water, a nest
> Out in the country and a place in Rome . . .

The question is never resolved.

Despite the optimism of its title, "Its Everlasting Possibility," the last section of the poem remains equally uncertain. With the instincts of a classicist, Pinsky sees the denial of limit as a "pride, or failing" common to all the races, classes, and regions of America. That denial may well be what transformed America from a republic to an empire. Vietnam ought finally to have taught America a lesson about limits.

> On television, I used to see, each week,
> Americans descending in machines

> With wasted bravery and blood; to spread
> Pain and vast fires amid a foreign place.
> . . . .
> I think it made our country older, forever.

Older, but not wiser. The lesson was not learned. A curious amalgam of "Nostalgia and Progress" continues to dominate the collective mind. No doubt every recent observer of America has been struck by the bizarre coexistence of an unlimited faith in technology with an assertion of what are imagined to be old-fashioned family and religious values. As Pinsky puts it,

> The country, boasting that it cannot see
> The past, waits dreaming ever of the past,
> Or all the plural pasts: the way a fetus
> Dreams vaguely of heaven.

Even the ageless mountains need protection, in the form of environmental laws, from the irresponsibility of technological somnambulism.

In the epilogue, the ambiguous tale of America is tacitly compared with Shakespeare's *Winter's Tale*. Hope may be reborn, despite appearances; the size and mobility of the country once again militate against a definitive conclusion. What can a classicist make of so unclassical a spectacle?

> Where nothing will stand still
> Nothing can end—but recoils into the past,
> Or is improvised into the dream or nightmare
> Romance of new beginnings.

A skeptical half-hope for the national future, by a mind that does not even know what it would be best to hope for, is the paradoxically patriotic conclusion to this uncertain explanation.

IF IT IS to be less ambiguous, the romance of new beginnings may have to be a private rather than a national renewal. The year after

163

Pinsky's poem was published, Ronald Reagan was elected president on the slogan "Together, a new beginning." It seems unlikely that Pinsky's hopes for his country or his daughter were advanced by such an appropriation, but there can be no doubt that the concept of new beginnings, on the level of advertising if not of poetry, had developed a mass appeal. The public consequences of that appeal are well known. For poets and thinkers, the most important effect was probably to intensify the division between public and private life that Richard Sennett described a decade ago in *The Fall of Public Man*. We shall be looking presently at one contemporary poet's jaundiced view of public life during the period when America was transforming itself into an imperial power. Before that, however, I want to examine a more private romance of new beginnings in Frederick Feirstein's *Manhattan Carnival* (1981), a poem whose exploration of American identity rarely becomes as explicit as Pinsky's and yet is perhaps, for that very reason, all the more searching and symptomatic.

If Pinsky's points of reference are on the whole classical, Feirstein's most immediately obvious ones are eighteenth-century and neoclassical. Like a satire of Pope's, the poem is written in heroic couplets, but its content and idiom are 1970s New York Jewish. To confuse matters further, the subtitle is *A Dramatic Monologue*. The poem's antecedents, like America's, are too various to fit it clearly into a single line of development. We might best think of it as a novel in verse that begins when Mark Stern, a New York playwright whose wife has left him, wakes up one morning and decides to rediscover himself.

> I shout into the mirror football cheers:
> "You've lived on this stone island thirty years
> And loved it for its faults; you are depressed.
> Get out, discover it again, get dressed."

If the city where he finds himself (in more senses than one) is not quite Whitman's "my own Manhattan," the search itself in its enthusiasm and inclusiveness is an expedition on which Whitman would have felt comfortable.

> My eye is like a child's; the smog is pot.
> Shining cratefuls of plum, peach, apricot
> Are flung out of the fruit man's tiny store.
> Behind the supermarket glass next door:
> Landslides of grapefruit, orange, tangerine,
> Persimmon, boysenberry, nectarine.
> The florist tilts his giant crayon box
> Of yellow roses, daffodils, and phlox.
> A Disney sun breaks through . . .

and on and on, a Whitman catalogue in which (*pace* Pinsky) Disney is as real and acceptable as daffodils, rock and roll as Mozart: contemporary America in the eye of the beholder.

There are no villains in *Manhattan Carnival*—how could such a frenetically inclusive work have villains?—but not all people and things arouse Mark Stern's sympathy equally. Landlords, bankers, sexual hypocrites, developers who destroy the urban landscape ("Helpless I watch as wreckers mug and rape / The Greek Revival houses. . . .") are bad but not inhuman. Children, and above all childlike adults, are good but not unflawed. Reviving the child in himself is one of Stern's goals; the child and the city are somehow bound together, and neither can be properly enjoyed without the other. In the simple plot of the poem, Stern's aim is to become childlike again partly for its own sake, partly so that his estranged wife Marlene will return to him. In ways that Robert Frost would have recognized, their lives have gone wrong; instead of being filled with wonder and enthusiasm, both of them were merely infantile.

> We lived inside a mirrored garbage can.
> Each day I grew more passive, you more wild.
> The child is only father of the child.

The solution, Stern feels, is to have a child of their own.

It must be obvious by now that Manhattan is more than a setting for this domestic drama. The exploration of self is also an exploration of the city-state; healing the self requires a new relation to the environment. That relation is always emotional and tactile, never political, as in earlier city-states. The mirrored garbage can has to become a carnival, not a *polis*. In that sense, we are still wandering in Pinsky's empire. However, variety and mobility are less threatening here than in Pinsky's poem. New York is filled with all kinds of people and things, many of them transient.

> A tourist wearing giveaway white gloves,
> A straw hat with a pin of turtle doves,
> Asks for the flavors in a Southern drawl.
> The ices-man snaps, "Just one left, that's all."
> "A typical New Yorker," she replies.
> Stunned by those words, tears welling in his eyes,
> He lifts her hand and kisses it. "For you
> —For free! dear lady, take my special brew."
> She sucks a cup of all his remnants mixed.
> A rainbow "Typical New York" has fixed.
> She walks away perplexed: is this one mad?
> He beams, "Two years an immigrant, not bad!"

Two kinds of Americans on the move encounter each other, are baffled, but make the best of it, more or less. It may not be an ideal way to create a nation, but there is no atrocity in it.

On the whole, the city is a good place, and people who reject it are rejecting themselves. To be sure, it has its frauds, financial and artistic. As in Pinsky, though to a much lesser extent, the American refusal to recognize limits leads, if not to catastrophe, at least to bad taste.

> The New World's paved with dog-shit, not with gold
> And tasteless in its art. These galleries
> Are filled with junk the touring Japanese
> Cart home with moccasins, tin Empire States,
> Key chains with footballs, paper license plates.

Nonetheless, the one point at which Stern momentarily repudiates the city is a moment of self-hatred:

> I hate this Spring, rebirth, no birth, this city.
> I hate my monomania, self-pity.
> I hate that Hasid, hate his button shop.
> I hate that jeweler, hate that traffic cop.
> I hate the Gotham Bookmart, Berger's Deli.

Only the most dehumanized monuments to greed, such as Sixth Avenue (officially the Avenue of the Americas) and the Hilton Hotel, deserve this reaction.

Manhattan, like life itself, is an opportunity for affirmation in this affirmative poem. Whatever our individual and collective histories may have done to us, however flawed or impaired we may be, carnival is still possible. The relatively optimistic conclusion of the poem is effective because so much stands in its way:

> In other words Corinna what I'm saying:
> We're crazy, wounded, but we are a-maying.

The poem ends with the Sterns apparently in the act of begetting a child to whom America may someday have to be explained anew, but one suspects that the explanation will be less skeptical and ironic than Pinsky's. Unlike *An Explanation of America, Manhattan Carnival* is rooted in a place whose identity is reasonably secure. Perhaps that limit to possibility allows the poet to be less threatened by the scale and transiency of life in contemporary America.

New York City, as most Americans will concede or proclaim, is not a typically American place; but then what is? The ancestors of most living Americans entered the New World through its harbor. The identity that Mark Stern discovers and the city in which it has meaning are as centrally American as any of the other selves that rot or flourish in what F. Scott Fitzgerald defined forever as the dark fields of the republic.

An Explanation of America and *Manhattan Carnival* might, in different senses, be described as poems of the Age of Carter, that humane season in which American introspection seemed to revive. Publicly and politically, if not poetically, it soon became evident that the reach of the new idealism exceeded its grasp. Robert Penn Warren's *Chief Joseph of the Nez Perce* is a poem for the harsher Age of Reagan, by which I mean not so much a harsher poem as one whose portrayal of American expansiveness and potential is bitterly ironic rather than even guardedly optimistic. The "atrocities" that Pinsky mentioned abstractly come to full historical life in this meditative narration about a nation of Indians, the Nez Perce of the Pacific Northwest, obliterated by a brutal notion of progress.

The most common use of history in modern poetry has been to comment on the present or on life in general, as in Pound's *Cantos* or Eliot's *Four Quartets*. American history, however, has several disadvantages as a central subject for narrative verse. First, nearly all of it is too recent, and therefore known in too much detail. Although it offers some highly dramatic episodes, they lend themselves better to novelistic treatment than to anything like traditional narrative poetry. The fact that the novel was already a well-developed literary form when the United States gained their independence has inhibited the development of American historical narratives in verse. Second, American history is on the whole too much of a success story to tempt the modern poetic mind. History usually takes on mythic qualities when it gets turned into poetry, and the most powerful myths are all of paradise lost. Victory and success have mythic properties only when achieved by underdogs, and it has been a long time since Americans were underdogs.

Warren would undoubtedly disagree with Pinsky that ignorance of limit is common to "all this country's regions, / Races, and classes." He would except the South. Ever since the South lost its war of independence, was devastated and conquered, its inhabitants have been more aware than other Americans that the strength and boldness of a people's aspirations do not guarantee their success. Warren has made a career of writing about the durable (though perhaps not unqualified) effects of defeat on the Southern mind; his most famous novel, *All the King's Men*, is a tragedy of political corruption and hubris in Louisiana.

It is hardly surprising that such a writer should turn his hand to one of the last of the Indian wars. *Chief Joseph of the Nez Perce*, published first by the *Georgia Review* in 1982 and then in an expanded version (from which I quote) in 1983, is narrated partly by the title character and partly by an omniscient, disillusioned modern. These two discordant voices sometimes threaten the poem's coherence, but for the most part the poem hangs together because the impersonal narrator's sympathies are so powerfully with the Indians. All of the poem's contemptuous irony is directed at the white characters and their descendants a century later.

In writing about the Nez Perce, Warren ascribes to them a Southern sense of the limits of self-assertion, a reverence for the earth and for their ancestors—in sharp contrast to the victorious Union veterans, insatiable conquerers of land and people, who defeat them. An advantage of writing about the traditional lives of Indians or other primitive peoples is that one can project upon them almost any set of attitudes one wishes. Their literary usefulness as a reflector of contemporary needs is unrivalled because so little is known about them. Warren has clearly mastered the few surviving records of the lives of the Nez Perce before their conquest; the mind of his Chief Joseph is an imaginative construct, however, that inevitably embodies historical realities less than the needs and anxieties of the present as Warren senses them.

Thus, at the beginning of the poem the Indians live in an Eden of nakedness, harmony with the natural world, truthfulness, and "unbridled glory."

> It is their land, and the bones of their fathers
> Yet love them, and in that darkness, lynxlike,

169

See how their sons still thrive without fear,
Not lying, not speaking with forkèd tongue.
Men know, in night-darkness, what wisdom thrives
    with the fathers.

In this paradise there are no serpents until the white men come, first in the form of French trappers, then Lewis and Clark, finally the United States Army and "the makers of treaties." Joseph's father signs the treaty of 1855 that guarantees the homeland of his people. For a time all is well. In 1873 President Grant again guarantees the land of Joseph's band; but the promise is not kept, and a few years later all the Nez Perce are ordered to a reservation. They fail to understand the white man's concept of truth and reality as determined by marks on paper that can be changed at will by other marks. Not only is their concept of truth different from the white man's; so is their idea of national identity. By this time Joseph's father has died and Joseph himself is chief, but throughout the poem he feels himself guided by his father's voice and watched by his father's eyes.

But then, my heart, it heard
My father's voice, like a great sky-cry
From snow-peaks in sunlight, and my voice
Was saying the Truth that no
White man can know, how the Great Spirit
Had made the earth but had drawn no lines
Of separation upon it, and all
Must remain as He made, for to each man
Earth is the Mother and Nurse, and to that spot
Where he was nursed, he must,
In love cling.

The greatest failing of white men in this poem, the flaw that motivates their brutality and greed, their perfidy and the corruptness of their public life, is their failure to love the land. For them, country and national identity are matters of documents and possession, not tradition and association—a frequent complaint of Southern writers about their Northern countrymen. America as a nation began, to be sure, with documents—the Declaration of Independence and the Constitution; the spontaneity of Joseph's feelings about his land has always been impossible for most white Americans. Ultimately the Indians fight for their land, the whites for gold and empire. Warren quotes a battlefield marker with bitter irony: "Before you . . . lies the historic battle ground of the Nez Perce Indian War in which 34 men gave their lives in service for their country." Whatever they gave their lives for, Warren seems to be saying, it was not "country" in any sense that the natives who were fighting for their homeland would have understood. The white men are found "clutching earth as though they had loved her" only after they have been killed.

The flaw of the white men is also their strength, and as the story unfolds in its inevitable way we are not surprised at the tactics by which they overcome Joseph's people. When two hostile nations track their way through mountains alien to both, the one trying to reach safety in Canada, the other trying to cut off escape, the winner is likely to be the one who understands maps and compasses. So it proves in this case, although the Indians' instincts for the land enable them to hold off white attacks more than once and almost, in the end, to make their escape. For a time the white soldiers are more brutal than effective.

> Near dawn they struck us, new horse-soldiers. Shot
> Into tepees. Women, children, old died.
> Some mothers might stand in the river's cold coil
> And hold up the infant and weep, and cry mercy.
> What heart beneath blue coat has fruited in mercy?
> When the slug plugged her bosom, unfooting her
> To the current's swirl and last darkness, what last
> Did she hear? It was laughter.

But we know, if we know anything at all about how the West was won, that eventually the soldiers will surround the Indians, that

171

the Indians will surrender after being promised to be allowed to return to their homeland, that the promise will be broken, that many of them will die of white men's diseases on a reservation. The "Sky-Chief" smiles on his worshippers for a time, then betrays them in an alien landscape. It is the endlessly depressing story of the Indians of the West.

Although the white men act in the service of impersonal history, not all of them are wholly depersonalized. General O. O. Howard lost an arm in the Civil War and feels himself driven by God's will and the love of glory. Colonel Miles, even more driven, flings his men across mountain ranges in the hope of capturing Joseph's band before Howard does. Their battle for reputation is with each other rather than with the Indians, who represent (to them) little more than a reproof and an opportunity. Both men are nearly demented with ambition. In the end, however, both draw back from their worst excesses. Arriving before the surrender, Howard sacrifices his longing:

> Stood there, commander, enduring the only
> Outlet of rage and hatred Miles
> Could give vent to: ironical courtesy, cold,
> Gray as snot. But Howard,
> Whose sweat had soaked sheets in wrestling with God,
> Laid his remaining hand on the steel-stiff shoulder
> That quivered beneath it. Howard, almost
> As soft as a whisper, promises him the surrender.
>
> And hearing his own words, he knew a pure
> And never-before-known bliss swell his heart.

Likewise Miles, his own ambition appeased, offers mercy to the Indians, and later even advocacy:

> And was it integrity, or some
> Sad division of self, torn in ambition
> And ambition's price, that at last made Miles

172

The only staunch friend of Joseph for all
The years? In his rising success, did something make Miles
Wonder what was the price of a star?

As at Appomattox, the conquerors are capable of mercy, charity, and ultimately some degree of self-knowledge. But the price of serving impersonal forces is irrelevance once one decides to stop serving them. Joseph wishes throughout to be a man in the eyes of his father. The eyes in whose gaze Howard and Miles perform—public opinion as expressed by newspapers—are not so easily placated. The Indians find that once he has befriended them, Miles carries no weight.

How could they know that Miles, whom they trusted,
Was only a brigadier behind whom
Move forces, faceless, timeless, dim,
And in such dimness, merciless?

Ambition, greed, and lust for empire are forces too powerful for mere Indians to stand in their way. Nor is any personal ideal of manhood a match for them. Heroes like Grant, Sherman, Howard, and Miles become figures of straw in the wind when they try to mitigate the destructiveness of their own victories. Brooding on his long-dead father and the destiny that has overtaken his own life, Joseph has the last word about men and nations:

But what is a man? An autumn-tossed aspen,
Pony-fart in the wind, the melting of snow-slush?
Yes, that is all. Unless—unless—
We can learn to live the Great Spirit's meaning
As the old and wise grope for it.

Glib and sentimental as this prescription may sound, Warren seems to be saying, it represents a wisdom beyond the grasp, let alone the practice, of the driven civilization that puts an end to the Nez Perce way of life and simultaneously to its own public virtues.

Except in those rare cases where it arises from attachment to a place, American identity is a matter of documents and pledges and rituals. In this conclusion Warren, Pinsky, and Feirstein would probably all agree. The Indians might have educated us in less destructive attitudes and ways of living, of being a people, if we had listened before we dispossessed them. Warren's poem reflects some light on the peculiar difficulties of writing successful narrative verse based on American history. Whether it points to any solution of those difficulties is more doubtful. History has certainly taken on qualities of myth here, a familiar primitivist myth, with all the problems of style and language that the use of such a myth raises in modern literature. Like Southerners, Warren's Nez Perce represent the pastoral victims of an abstract, implacable American destiny. They even get beaten by the same men. (Of course, white Southerners are less amenable to this kind of idealization: they helped displace the Indians, they kept slaves, and they left more records of themselves.) When it comes to the making or maintaining of a national self, W. H. Auden put it most memorably:

> History to the defeated
> May say Alas but cannot help or pardon.

Poets, likewise, can do no more than explore and try to explain.

In a recent essay, James Laughlin described Pound's earlier *Cantos* as a narrative interweaving of such "disparate lives" as Confucius, Malatesta, Jefferson, and went on to maintain that "their stories comment on one another; the process becomes a kind of moral criticism."[4] The poems I have just been discussing are more conventionally organized than the *Cantos*—indeed, the several kinds of long poem they represent might all be regarded as repudiations of Pound's technique—but the same comment could be applied to them all. Moral criticism is not just something imposed from outside by a reader; it often inheres, as I said at the beginning of this book, in the very structure of literary works themselves. That inherence is its most important justification as a critical practice. At the highest degree of literary intensity, the moralist becomes a prophet, an altogether less comfortable figure but one who has fared better with recent critics.

To ignore in our reading the ethical significance of poems and novels is to close our eyes to something that many poets and novelists have considered central in their imaginative purposes. It is also, quite simply, an unnatural way to read. Moral categories and intentions may be analyzed in a variety of ways, in literature as in politics and everyday life. We need not, of course, take all intentions at face value—or, more shallow still, take the intention for the literary achievement. Faults like these have sometimes made moral criticism seem narrow or merely naive. They have not, however, made it dispensable. At the most, they have driven critics to disguise moral observations in the terminology of esthetics, politics, or psychoanalysis. To take only one example, the discussions of "canon formation" that have become such a feature of contemporary critical debate would be more honest, and therefore perhaps more profitable, if all parties recognized that the issues are at bottom moral rather than historical. To conclude that they thereby lose their status as literary issues is to approach literature with tunnel vision.

W. H. Auden, whom I have quoted above on the subject of history, is all too well known for the aphorism "Poetry makes nothing happen." Less often cited is the following passage from his introduction to *The Poet's Tongue* (1935):

> The propagandist, whether moral or political, complains that the writer should use his powers over words to persuade people to a particular course of action, instead of fiddling while Rome burns. But Poetry is not concerned with telling people what to do, but with extending our knowledge of good and evil, perhaps making the necessity for action more urgent and its nature more clear, but only leading us to the point where it is possible for us to make a rational and moral choice.[5]

175

To succeed in these tasks is, of course, to make something happen. In its balance of modesty and assertiveness, Auden's statement would have been accepted by most of the writers I have examined in this book, despite their manifest differences. There seems little evidence that Poe, Wilde, or Derrida have lessened most writers' confidence in their ability to illuminate ethical questions through the practice of their art.

Literary critics are another matter. Tzvetan Todorov has forcefully restated the critical counterpart of Auden's ambitions for poetry. His formulation offers a promising note on which to close:

> The question, "What does this text mean?" is a relevant one, and we must still try to answer it, without discarding any context—historical, structural or other—which can assist us in this task. For all that, one need not stop there: another, twofold question can be addressed to the answer of the former one: "Is it true? And is it right?" In this way, we might transcend the sterile dichotomy between specialist critics who know but do not think, and moralist critics who speak while not knowing much about the works of literature they speak about. And the literary critic might begin at last to play the role he has always been intended to play, that of a participant in a double dialogue: as reader, with his author; as author, with his own readers—who, in that event, might even be more numerous.[6]

Notes

1. Morality, Poetry, and Criticism

1. Denis Donoghue, *New York Times Book Review,* 24 January 1982, p. 20.

2. I. A. Richards, *Poetries and Sciences* (New York: Norton, 1970), p. 33. Richards is emphasizing here the psychological causes and effects of poetic language.

3. Cleanth Brooks, *The Well Wrought Urn* (New York: Harcourt, Brace, 1947), p. 256. The moral consequences of a purely esthetic view of poetry are well stated by Paul J. Marcotte: "A piece of literature is a thing, a fine artifact; it is not a *human act.* A piece of literature is the result of a human act. Consequently, a piece of literature, viewed as literature, cannot be either morally good or morally evil. . . . To speak of a morally bad piece of literature is as foolish as to speak of a morally bad table or chair" (*The God Within* [Ottawa: Hiamaska, 1964], p. 104).

4. See E. D. Hirsch, *The Aims of Interpretation* (Chicago: University of Chicago Press, 1976), especially chapters 7 and 8, for a discussion of "extrinsic" and "intrinsic" criteria to which I am indebted. For a general discussion of poetry and ideas, see Gerald Graff, *Poetic Statement and Critical Dogma* (Chicago: University of Chicago Press, 1970), and my *The Place of Poetry* (Lexington: University Press of Kentucky, 1981), especially chapter 1. Poetic truth is not, of course, always or only moral. Nor, where it is descriptive truth, can it always be formulated propositionally.

5. Wayne C. Booth, *Critical Understanding: The Powers and Limits of Pluralism* (Chicago: University of Chicago Press, 1979), p. 363, note 18; see also his *Modern Dogma and the Rhetoric of Assent* (Notre Dame: Notre Dame University Press, 1974), appendix B. For a scientist who takes a

similar view, see Jacob Bronowski, *The Origins of Knowledge and Imagination* (New Haven: Yale University Press, 1978), pp. 127–33.

6. It has sometimes been asserted that there is a "poetic ethics," a set of values to which great poets of all ages have subscribed. The idea is not quite as far-fetched as it sounds; its truth or falsity, like the question of the source of moral values, is beyond the scope of this essay. For a defense of it, see Charles A. Dinsmore, *The Great Poets and the Meaning of Life* (1937; rpt. Freeport, New York: Books for Libraries Press, 1968), pp. 243ff.

7. Sir Philip Sidney, *Defence of Poetry*, ed. J. A. Van Dorsten (London: Oxford University Press, 1966), pp. 34, 29. Tolstoy, in "What Is Art?" (1898), states a similar position: "The business of art lies just in this: to make that understood and felt which in the form of an argument might be incomprehensible and inaccessible. Usually it seems to the recipient of a truly artistic impression that he knew the thing before, but had been unable to express it" (quoted from Richard Ellmann and Charles Feidelson, Jr., eds., *The Modern Tradition* [New York: Oxford University Press, 1965], p. 305).

8. Samuel Johnson, "John Milton," in *Lives of the English Poets*, ed. G. B. Hill (Oxford: Clarendon Press, 1905), vol. 1, pp. 99–100. In an important and unfortunately neglected book directed against Richards' "emotive" theory of poetic language, William Empson argues for a cognitive and moral view that has much in common with both Johnson's and my own; for example, "The sort of truth we are shown [in a poem], in which we find ourselves believing, is one about our own natures and the natures of the other people we have to deal with; perhaps it is essentially no more than the truth that to act in some ways would be good, and in others bad. Dr. Johnson, one can suppose, would have been ready to limit it to that" (*The Structure of Complex Words* [Norfolk, Conn.: New Directions, n.d.], p. 9).

9. René Wellek and Austin Warren, *Theory of Literature*, 3rd rev. ed. (London: Jonathan Cape, 1966), p. 35.

10. Laurence Lerner, *The Truest Poetry* (London: Hamish Hamilton, 1960), p. 5.

11. John Gardner, *On Moral Fiction* (New York: Basic Books, 1978), p. 6.

12. "Religion and Literature" (1935), in Frank Kermode, ed., *Selected Prose of T. S. Eliot* (New York: Harcourt, Brace, 1975), p. 97.

13. George Watson, *Modern Literature and Thought* (Heidelberg: Winter, 1978), p. 36. The best statement I know of the relation between form and content from this point of view remains G. B. Shaw's Epistle Dedicatory to *Man and Superman*.

14. Hirsch, *The Aims of Interpretation*, pp. 2–3. Later in the same chapter, Hirsch goes on to say: "The recent overemphasis on aesthetic values in literature has had a restrictive and inhibiting effect on literary criticism and literary study. The aesthetic conception of literature has too rigidly limited the canon of literature and has too narrowly confined the scope of literary study, leaving present-day scholars with little to do that is at once 'legitimate' and important" (12).

2. Death and Two Maidens

1. Quoted in George Watson, *The Discipline of English* (London: Macmillan, 1978), p. 79.

2. Johan Huizinga, *Homo Ludens* (Boston: Beacon Press, 1955), p. 45.

3. Richard Sennett, *The Fall of Public Man* (New York: Knopf, 1977), p. 266.

4. Huizinga, *Homo Ludens*, p. 3.

5. Lewis Carroll, *Alice in Wonderland*, ed. Donald J. Gray (New York: Norton, 1971), p. 162. All quotations from Carroll are from this edition and will henceforth be cited parenthetically. The archaic double apostrophe in *can't* and *won't* has been silently modernized.

6. Sennett, *The Fall of Public Man*, p. 11.

7. Ibid., p. 267.

3. Home and Away

1. Peter Green, *Kenneth Grahame: A Biography* (London: Murray, 1959), p. 202.

2. Kenneth Grahame, *The Wind in the Willows* (1908; rpt. London: Methuen, 1960), p. 127. All quotations hereafter will be identified parenthetically in the text.

3. Samuel L. Clemens, *Adventures of Huckleberry Finn* (1885; rpt. New York: Norton, 1977), p. 7. All quotations hereafter will be identified parenthetically in the text.

4. Geraldine D. Poss, "An Epic in Arcadia: The Pastoral World of *The Wind in the Willows,*" *Children's Literature* 4 (1975): 81. Poss considers interestingly the question of whether *The Wind in the Willows* is really a children's book and arrives at a negative conclusion based on the difficulty of its vocabulary and "the longing for a golden age" which it embodies. But some children do long for golden ages, and the vocabulary was less difficult in the England of 1908.

5. Home, of course, may represent many different values in books for either children or adults, but it is noteworthy that the security of a conventional family is not available to the main characters of any of the books I am discussing. Nor do any of them seem to miss it. Huck, Rat, Toad, Mole, Bilbo, and Frodo are all permanently celibate, and the only surviving parent any of them has is Pap Finn. For a very different treatment of "homes" in *The Wind in the Willows,* see Lois R. Kuznets, "Toad Hall Revisited," *Children's Literature* 7(1978): 115−28.

6. J. R. R. Tolkien, "On Fairy-Stories," in *The Tolkien Reader* (New York: Ballantine Books, 1966), p. 60.

7. Like *The Wind in the Willows, The Hobbit* was first told to and then written for children; it also possesses the rarer distinction of having been accepted for publication by a ten-year-old. See Humphrey Carpenter, *Tolkien* (Boston: Houghton Mifflin, 1977), pp. 180−81.

8. J. R. R. Tolkien, *The Fellowship of the Ring* (Boston: Houghton Mifflin, 1965), p. 93.

9. J. R. R. Tolkien, *The Return of the King* (Boston: Houghton Mifflin, 1965), p. 309.

10. Not in the story itself, at least. The fact that Sam has a wife and child when Frodo departs, and plays an adult role in governing the Shire, merely makes him a more conventional character than Frodo, not a mature one. As his age and social status increase, Sam evidently comes to share Frodo's outlook. The appendices tell us that after raising his children and serving as Mayor for many years, he too leaves the Shire and passes over the sea (*Return of the King,* p. 378).

4. Sherlock Holmes, Order, and
the Late-Victorian Mind

1. Sir Arthur Conan Doyle, *The Complete Sherlock Holmes*, 2 vols. (New York: Doubleday, n.d.). All quotations from the Holmes stories are from this, the standard American edition, and are identified by volume and page in parentheses. In citing the titles of stories, I have consistently omitted "The Adventure of" for the sake of conciseness.

2. Thomas Love Peacock, "An Essay on Fashionable Literature" (1818), in H. F. B. Brett-Smith and C. E. Jones, eds., *The Works of Thomas Love Peacock* (rpt., New York: AMS Press, 1967), vol. 8, p. 265.

3. Geoffrey Best, *Mid-Victorian Britain 1851–1875* (New York: Schocken Books, 1972), p. 270. One of Best's illustrations (fig. 5) shows "one of the guarded gates which protected so many superior-class residential streets and squares."

4. That is, if one accepts Doyle's view of the Mormons as a secret society. The preoccupation with secret societies had a long history, as Marilyn Butler points out:

> After the French Revolution . . . the conservative imagination . . . becomes possessed by the idea of an evil conspiracy. The secret societies of the period become less clearly defined and perhaps even more terrifying a band of dedicated fanatics bent on drawing the innocent into their clutches as a step toward augmenting their power and influence. The fascination felt by writers of all opinions for secret societies, identified or not identified, contemporary or historical, is a symptom of the instability and political hysteria felt throughout Europe in the 1790's. (*Jane Austen and the War of Ideas* [Oxford: Clarendon Press, 1975], p. 115)

The revived literary interest in such societies a century later had something to do with the rise of anarchism; perhaps the chief literary monument to that interest is G. K. Chesterton's *The Man Who Was Thursday* (1908). See James Joll, *The Anarchists* (Cambridge, Mass.: Harvard University Press, 1979).

5. Julian Symons, *Mortal Consequences* (New York: Schocken Books, 1973), p. 10.

6. Ibid., pp. 10–11, 65. Pierre Nordon makes a similar series of points in *Conan Doyle* (New York: Holt, Rinehart, 1967), especially chapter 14.

Like Nordon, Erik Routley, in *The Puritan Pleasures of the Detective Story* (London: Gollancz, 1972), sees Holmes as a figure of chivalric romance updated for the late nineteenth century. As Routley puts it, "Holmes is what he is because of the counterpoint between the character of the cold logical reasoner and the romantic remoteness of this character from the ordinary run of fictional heroes" (42). The word *romantic* in this formulation strikes me as lacking precision.

7. George Watson, *The English Ideology: Studies in the Language of Victorian Politics* (London: Allen Lane, 1973).

8. Stephen Knight, *Form and Ideology in Crime Fiction* (London: Macmillan, 1980), p. 87.

9. J. J. Tobias, *Crime and Police in England 1700–1900* (Dublin: Gill and Macmillan, 1979), pp. 145, 146.

10. Ibid., pp. 57ff.

11. Ibid., p. 73; cf. Best, *Mid-Victorian Britain*, p. 271.

12. Tobias, *Crime and Police*, pp. 159–70. Transportation to the American colonies began soon after the settlement at Jamestown; the Virginia General Assembly protested the practice as early as 1670, but it continued until the colonies rebelled in 1775. Tobias estimates that some fifty thousand convicts were eventually sent to America (162). From 1785 until the early 1850s Australia was used. Convict colonies were about as popular as nuclear-waste dumps today, and when the Australians declared their country off limits, the British government finally called it quits and built more prisons at home.

13. Francis Thompson's poem "The Hound of Heaven," in which the canine pursuer represented a very different supernatural intrusion into civilized life, had appeared in 1893.

14. G. M. Trevelyan, in his *English Social History* (New York: David McKay, 1942), optimistically dates this process back to the 1850s (530–31). But as Geoffrey Best makes clear (*Mid-Victorian Britain*, p. 271), it took a long time to become a reality. Furthermore, in 1877 the Detective Department of Scotland Yard "lost all its credibility in the eyes of both police and public" when three of its four chief detective inspectors were involved in a bribery scandal; in the following year, the modern Criminal Investigation Department was created (Tobias, *Crime and Police*, p. 112).

15. As I discovered after finishing this essay, Ian Ousby speculates along similar lines in *Bloodhounds of Heaven: The Detective in English Fiction from Godwin to Doyle* (Cambridge, Mass.: Harvard University Press, 1976), pp. 173–75.

16. I. F. Clarke, *Voices Prophesying War* (London: Oxford University Press, 1966), pp. 3, 68–69.

17. Edmund Wilson put the same distinction another way in 1945: "My contention is that Sherlock Holmes *is* literature on a humble but not ignoble level, whereas the mystery writers most in vogue now are not" (*Classics and Commercials* [New York: Farrar, Straus, 1950], p. 267). Wilson is one of the few well-known critics to have discussed the Holmes stories as literature; unfortunately he did so very briefly.

5. J. R. R. Tolkien: The Monsters and the Critics

1. C. S. Lewis, "The Dethronement of Power," reprinted in Neil D. Isaacs and Rose A. Zimbardo, eds., *Tolkien and the Critics* (Notre Dame: University of Notre Dame Press, 1968), p. 16.

2. W. H. Auden, "The Quest Hero," reprinted in Isaacs and Zimbardo, *Tolkien and the Critics*, p. 61.

3. Edmund Wilson, "Oo, Those Awful Orcs!" reprinted in his *The Bit between My Teeth* (New York: Farrar, Straus, 1966), pp. 329–32.

4. Humphrey Carpenter, *Tolkien* (Boston: Houghton Mifflin, 1977), p. 223.

5. J. R. R. Tolkien, *The Fellowship of the Ring,* rev. ed. (Boston: Houghton Mifflin, 1965), p. 7. The point is repeated in a number of letters. All quotations from *Lord of the Rings* are taken from the edition of which this is the first volume and are cited parenthetically by volume and page number.

6. Humphrey Carpenter, ed., *The Letters of J. R. R. Tolkien* (Boston: Houghton Mifflin, 1981), pp. 178–79.

7. As published in *The Tolkien Reader* (New York: Ballantine Books, 1966), esp. pp. 9–10.

8. Catharine R. Stimpson, *J. R. R. Tolkien* (New York: Columbia University Press, 1969); Burton Raffel, "*The Lord of the Rings* as Literature," in Isaacs and Zimbardo, *Tolkien and the Critics*, pp. 218–46.

9. Robert Giddings, ed., *J. R. R. Tolkien: This Far Land* (London: Vision Press, 1983), p. 19.

10. Carpenter, *Letters,* pp. 189, 194.

11. Ibid., p. 197.

12. Ibid., p. 215.

13. In this as in most respects, Tolkien was conscious of what he was doing, even if he sometimes miscalculated the effects. For his defense of archaisms in *Lord of the Rings,* see Carpenter, *Letters,* pp. 225–26.

14. Nick Otty, "The Structuralist's Guide to Middle-earth," in Giddings, *J. R. R. Tolkien,* p. 178.

15. George Orwell, *1984* (New York: New American Library, 1961), pp. 205, 218.

16. "All against Humanity," *Times Literary Supplement,* 4 October 1985, pp. 1093–94.

17. Orwell, *1984,* p. 220.

18. Carpenter, *Letters,* p. 211. In a subsequent comment on Auden's review of *The Return of the King,* Tolkien declared: "I have not made any of the peoples on the 'right' side, Hobbits, Rohirrim, Men of Dale or of Gondor, any better than men have been or are, or can be. Mine is not an 'imaginary' world, but an imaginary historical moment on 'Middle-earth'—which is our habitation" (Carpenter, *Letters,* p. 244).

6. Robert Frost's Marriage Group

1. Yvor Winters, "Robert Frost: Or, the Spiritual Drifter as Poet," reprinted in James M. Cox, ed., *Robert Frost: A Collection of Critical Essays* (Englewood Cliffs: Prentice Hall, 1962), p. 82.

2. Dates (which are those of first publication) and quotations are all from Edward Connery Lathem, ed., *The Poetry of Robert Frost* (New York: Holt, Rinehart, 1969).

3. *Robert Frost: The Work of Knowing* (New York: Oxford University Press, 1977), p. 223.

7. Padraic Pearse: The Revolutionary as Artist

1. George Bernard Shaw, *John Bull's Other Island . . .* (London: Constable, 1911), p. 18. The most thorough account of Shaw's changing atti-

tudes toward Irish nationalism is Stanley Weintraub, "The Making of an Irish Patriot," *Eire/Ireland* 5 (1970): 9–27.

2. His writings on the Dublin transport strike, for example, make this clear. See, for example, Padraic H. Pearse, *Political Writings and Speeches* (*Collected Works of Padraic H. Pearse*, vol. 1 [Dublin: Phoenix, n.d.]), pp. 171–81.

3. For example, William Irwin Thompson, *The Imagination of an Insurrection* (New York: Oxford University Press, 1967), pp. 115, 125, 207; Edward Malins, *Yeats and the Easter Rising* (Dublin: Dolmen Press, 1965), pp. 23–24. Both writers see Pearse's political acts as those of a frustrated artist. See also Raymond Porter, *P. H. Pearse* (New York: Twayne, 1973).

4. Pearse, *Political Writings*, pp. 365–66.

5. Ibid., p. 221.

6. Ibid., p. 144. Although no name is mentioned, the reference is almost certainly to Yeats.

7. Ibid., pp. 53–54.

8. Ibid., pp. 300–301.

9. Padraic H. Pearse, *Plays, Stories, Poems* (*Collected Works of Padraic H. Pearse*, vol. 2 [Dublin: Phoenix, n.d.]), p. 315. Further quotations from this volume will be cited parenthetically in the text.

10. In *The Story of a Success* (*Collected Works of Padraic H. Pearse*, vol. 4 [Dublin: Phoenix, n.d.], pp. 76–77), Pearse recounts a dream that he seems to have had in 1909:

> I dreamt that I saw a pupil of mine, one of our boys at St. Enda's, standing alone upon a platform above a mighty sea of people; and I understood that he was about to die there for some august cause, Ireland's or another. . . . The great silent crowd regarded the boy with pity and wonder rather than with approval—as a fool who was throwing away his life rather than a martyr that was doing his duty. It would have been so easy to die before an applauding crowd or before a hostile crowd: but to die before that silent unsympathetic crowd! . . . This is the only really vivid dream I have ever had since I used to dream of hobgoblins when I was a child.

11. Even the day of the rising had prospective significance (beyond the religious), for Pearse points out that "the Irish, come down from the mountains, annihilated the Bristol colonists of Dublin on Easter Monday, 1209; whence Easter Monday was known in Dublin as Black Monday"

(*Story of a Success*, p. 4). The first site of St. Enda's School, Cullenswood House, overlooked the fields where the massacre had occurred.

12. Weintraub, "The Making of an Irish Patriot," pp. 17–18.

13. Reprinted in George Bernard Shaw, *The Matter with Ireland*, ed. David H. Greene and Dan H. Laurence (London: Hart-Davis, 1962), p. 113. In the same letter, perhaps thinking of Pearse, he declared, "It is absolutely impossible to slaughter a man in this position without making him a martyr and a hero, even though the day before the rising he may have been only a minor poet" (ibid., p. 112).

14. Archibald Henderson, *George Bernard Shaw: Man of the Century* (New York: Appleton-Century-Crofts, 1956), p. 302. After the executions, Shaw's feelings were much like those of Yeats: "I never felt so morose in my life" (letter to Mrs. Patrick Campbell, 14 May 1916, quoted by Weintraub, p. 21).

15. His actions and writings were hardly a contribution to the peaceful reunion of his country. The following passage, written in November 1913, is an example of his approach to North-South relations:

> I am glad, then, that the North has "begun." I am glad that the Orangemen have armed, for it is a goodly thing to see arms in Irish hands. . . . I should like to see any and every body of Irish citizens armed. We must accustom ourselves to the thought of arms, to the sight of arms, to the use of arms. We may make mistakes in the beginning and shoot the wrong people; but bloodshed is a cleansing and a sanctifying thing, and the nation which regards it as the final horror has lost its manhood. (*Political Writings*, pp. 98–99)

This passage is similar to one in which Shaw expressed himself on civil war in Ireland: "I do not deprecate that method; for if hatred, calumny, and terror have so possessed men that they cannot live in peace as other nations do, they had better fight it out and get rid of their bad blood that way" (quoted by Weintraub, p. 27). It needs to be added that Shaw did not believe civil war likely and did not look forward to the prospect with eagerness; nevertheless, with these qualifications, we have another example of the way Pearse, through action, imposed something like his own state of mind on greater writers.

8. *Czeslaw Milosz: The Exile as Californian*

1. *Selected Poems,* of which the most recent edition was published by Ecco Press in 1980, is one of only two volumes of Milosz's poetry that have so far appeared in English. The other is *Bells in Winter,* published by Ecco in 1978. Except where otherwise indicated, all of my verse quotations are from *Selected Poems.*

9. *Explorations of America*

1. Dana Gioia, "The Dilemma of the Long Poem," *Kenyon Review,* n.s., 5 (Spring 1983): 19, 22.

2. Robert Pinsky, *An Explanation of America* (Princeton: Princeton University Press, 1979); Frederick Feirstein, *Manhattan Carnival: A Dramatic Monologue* (Woodstock, Vt.: Countryman Press, 1981); Robert Penn Warren, *Chief Joseph of the Nez Perce, Who Called Themselves the Nimipu, "The Real People"* (New York: Random House, 1983).

3. Robert Pinsky, *The Situation of Poetry* (Princeton: Princeton University Press, 1976), p. 162.

4. *New York Times Book Review,* 10 November 1985, p. 58.

5. Edward Mendelson, ed., *The English Auden* (New York: Random House, 1977), p. 329.

6. *Times Literary Supplement,* 4 October 1985, p. 1094.

Index